WHAT A W🌐RLD 2
LISTENING

Amazing Stories
from Around the Globe

Milada Broukal

PEARSON
Longman

What a World Listening 2: Amazing Stories from Around the Globe

Pearson Education, 10 Bank Street, White Plains, NY 10606 USA

Staff credits: The people who made up the *What a World Listening 2* team, representing editorial, production, design, and manufacturing, are Pietro Alongi, Rhea Banker, John Brezinsky, Andrea Bryant, Aerin Csigay, Gina DiLillo, Nancy Flaggman, Oliva Fernandez, Lisa Ghiozzi, Amy McCormick, Linda Moser, Jennifer Stem, and Patricia Wosczyk.
Cover and text design: Patricia Wosczyk
Text composition: ElectraGraphics, Inc.
Text font: Minion
Photo Credits: Cover, David Noton/Getty Images; Page 1, Ian Shaw/Alamy; p. 4, (left) Shutterstock.com, (right) Shutterstock.com; p. 8, Shutterstock.com; p. 10, (left) Shutterstock.com, (right) Shutterstock.com; p. 14, Henry Westheim Photography/Alamy; p. 17, (left) Dreamstime.com, (right) Andrea Rossi/EIDON/MAXPPP/Newscom; p. 21, Shutterstock.com; p. 23, (left) Shutterstock.com, (right) Shutterstock.com; p. 28, Shutterstock.com; p. 36, Shutterstock.com; p. 39, (left) Shutterstock.com, (right) Shutterstock.com; p. 43, Dreamstime.com; p. 46, (left) Shutterstock.com, (right) Shutterstock.com; p. 50, Shutterstock.com; p. 53, (left) Shutterstock.com, (right) Shutterstock.com; p. 58, Shutterstock.com; p. 61, (left) Photos 12/Alamy, (right) Shutterstock.com; p. 70, Shutterstock.com; p. 73, (left) Shutterstock.com, (right) Shutterstock.com; p. 77, Judy Eddy/WENN/Newscom; p. 80, (left) Kent Meireis/The Image Works, (right) Shutterstock.com; p. 85, Shutterstock.com; p. 88, (left) Shutterstock.com, (right) Shutterstock.com; p. 92, Photos 12/Alamy; p. 95, (left) Lebrecht Music and Arts Photo Library/Alamy, (right) Lebrecht Music and Arts Photo Library/Alamy; p. 99, Shutterstock.com; p. 102, (left) Shutterstock.com, (right) Shutterstock.com; p. 107, Shutterstock.com; p. 110, (left) Shutterstock.com, (right) Shutterstock.com; p. 114, Dreamstime.com; p. 117, (left) Shutterstock.com, (right) Mirek Hejnicki/Fotolia.com; p. 122, Dreamstime.com; p. 130, Shutterstock.com

Library of Congress Cataloging-in-Publication Data

Broukal, Milada.
  What a world listening : amazing stories from around the globe / Milada Broukal.
     p. cm.—(What a world listening : amazing stories from around the globe series)
  Previously published as: What a world, 2004.
  ISBN 0-13-247389-5 (v. 1)—ISBN 0-13-247795-5 (v. 2)—ISBN 0-13-138200-4
(v. 3) 1. English language—Textbooks for foreign speakers. 2. Listening. I. Title.
  PE1128.B717 2010
  428.2'4—dc21

                                                                2010037494

ISBN-13: 978-0-13-247795-6
ISBN-10: 0-13-247795-5

PEARSON LONGMAN ON THE WEB

Pearsonlongman.com offers online resources for teachers and students. Access our Companion Websites, our online catalog, and our local offices around the world.

Visit us at **www.pearsonlongman.com**.

Printed in the United States of America
5 6 7 8 9 10–V011–14 13

CONTENTS

UNIT	VOCABULARY	LANGUAGE FOCUS	PRONUNCIATION
1 **WHAT ARE SOME DIFFERENT TYPES OF INVENTIONS?** PAGES **1–7**	*base • fan • floats • items • keyboard • magnet • screen • supports* *alarm clock • goes off • in reality*	Simple Present with Adverbs of Frequency	Word Stress: Adverbs of Frequency
2 **WHAT IS BEAUTY AROUND THE WORLD?** PAGES **8–13**	*complexion • elaborate • features • full • ideals • shiny • status • trendy* *a sign of • inner beauty • pop celebrities*	Order of Adjectives	Word Stress: Adjective + Noun Combinations
3 **WHAT COUNTRIES HAVE ROYALTY TODAY?** PAGES **14–20**	*accommodates • affluent • astounding • browsing • excessive • fortune • monarchies • resources* *estimated value • gold-plated • well off*	Comparative and Superlative Adjectives	Word Stress: Superlative Adjectives
4 **WHAT ARE SOME RITES OF PASSAGE?** PAGES **21–27**	*attach • elastic • feat • leap • novice • occur • procession • ritual* *participate in • take place • take turns*	*Before* and *After* in Time Clauses	Vowel Sounds: *dive* /aɪ/, *wish*/ɪ/, and *leap* /i/
5 **WHO ARE SOME FAMOUS EXPLORERS?** PAGES **28–35**	*assignments • boundary • challenging • encounters • endured • expedition • hardships • hostile* *intrigued by • lost civilizations • were about to*	Simple Past	Vowel Sounds: *book* /ʊ/ and *food* /u/
6 **WHAT ARE SOME JOBS THAT ARE UNIQUE TO AUSTRALIA?** PAGES **36–42**	*allow • bait • capture • endangered • harbor • jaws • mean • trained* *go for it • rely on • set a trap*	The Conditional with the Present and the Past	*-er* and *-or* Endings

INTRODUCTION

What a World: Amazing Stories from Around the Globe—the series

This series now has two strands: a listening strand and a reading strand. Both strands explore linked topics from around the world and across history. They can be used separately or together for maximum exploration of content and development of essential listening and reading skills.

	Listening Strand	**Reading Strand**
Level 1 (Beginning)	*What a World Listening 1*	*What a World Reading 1, 2e*
Level 2 (High-Beginning)	*What a World Listening 2*	*What a Word Reading 2, 2e*
Level 3 (Intermediate)	*What a World Listening 3*	*What a Word Reading 3, 2e*

What a World Listening 2—a high-beginning listening and speaking skills book

It is the second in a three-book series of listening and speaking skills for English language learners. The eighteen units in this book correspond thematically with the units in *What a World Reading 2, 2e*. Each topic is about a different person, society, animal, place, custom, or organization. The topics span history and the globe, from what the Chinese gave us, to famous detective story characters, to where people live the longest.

Unit Structure and Approach

BEFORE YOU LISTEN opens with a picture of the person, society, animal, place, custom, or organization featured in the unit. Prelistening questions follow. Their purpose is to motivate students to listen, encourage predictions about the content of the listening, and involve the students' own experiences when possible. Vocabulary can be presented as the need arises.

LONG TALK can be any one of a variety of scenarios, including a class lecture, a long conversation between two people, or a tour guide speaking to a group. The talk is generally about 300–350 words long. After an initial listening for general content, the teacher may wish to explain the words in the vocabulary section. The students should then do a second, closer listening, perhaps in chunks. Further listening can be done depending on the students' requirements.

VOCABULARY exercises focus on the important topic-related words in the long talk. Both *Meaning* and *Words That Go Together* are definition exercises that encourage students to work out the meanings of words from the context. *Meaning* focuses on single words, *Words That Go Together* focuses on collocations or groups of words which are easier to learn together the way they are used in the language. The third exercise, *Use*, reinforces the vocabulary further by making students use the words or collocations in a meaningful, yet possibly different, context. This section can be done during or after the listening to the long talk, or both.

COMPREHENSION exercises appear in each unit and consist of *Understanding the Listening* and *Remembering Details*. These confirm the content of the talk either in general or in detail. These exercises for developing listening skills can be done individually, in pairs, in small groups, or as a class. It is preferable to do these exercises in conjunction with the long talk, since they are not meant to test memory.

TAKING NOTES is a fun feature where students listen to a short description of a place, person, or thing related to the unit. It is not necessary for students to understand every word, but they are encouraged to take notes. From their notes, they decide which of the two options they are given fits the description.

SHORT CONVERSATIONS consists of three new conversations related to the topic of the unit. The exercises focus on content as well as the speaker's tone and attitude, what the speaker is doing, the speaker's job, and where the conversation is taking place.

DISCUSSION questions encourage students to bring their own ideas to the related topics in each long talk. They can also provide insights into cultural similarities and differences.

CRITICAL THINKING questions give students the opportunity to develop thinking skills (comparing and contrasting cultural customs, recognizing personal attitudes and values, etc.).

LANGUAGE FOCUS draws on a grammatical structure from the listening and offers exercises to help students develop accuracy in speaking and writing. The exercises build from controlled to more open-ended.

PRONUNCIATION exercises focus on a recurring pronunciation feature in the unit. These exercises help students to hear and practice word endings, reductions, stress, and intonation.

CONVERSATION exercises start with a set conversation for students to listen to and repeat. Then students progress to a freer conversation that they create using new expressions from the set conversations.

Additional Activities

INTERNET ACTIVITIES (in the Appendices) help students develop their Internet research skills. Each activity can be done in a classroom setting or if the students have Internet access, as homework leading to a presentation or discussion in class. There is an Internet activity for each unit and it is always related to the theme of the unit. It helps students evaluate websites for their reliability and gets them to process and put together the information in an organized way.

SELF-TESTS after Unit 9 and Unit 18 review general listening comprehension, vocabulary, and the grammar from the language focus in a multiple-choice format.

＊＊＊＊＊

The **Answer Key** for *What a World Listening 2* is available at the following website: http://www.pearsonlongman.com/whataworld.

WHAT ARE SOME DIFFERENT TYPES OF INVENTIONS?

before you listen

Answer these questions.

1. What is the most important invention in the last 1,000 years? Why?

2. What is the most important invention in the last ten years? Why?

3. What is an invention you don't like? Why?

VOCABULARY

MEANING

Listen to the talk. Then write the correct words in the blanks.

base	floats	keyboard	screen
fan	items	magnet	supports

1. It's hard to type on my new _____ because it's very small.

2. I got a new _____ to keep my room cool in the summer.

3. My sister made an invention for her science fair that uses a(n) _____ to pick up paperclips from the floor.

4. I would love to see an invention that has a plastic _____ to hold a knife and fork in place on the table.

5. The picture on my new computer _____ is very sharp and clear.

6. I am surprised that just one piece of wood _____ such a big table.

7. There are always a lot of interesting _____ at the Young Inventors' Fair.

8. An interesting invention is a bed that stays in the air. It _____ above the floor!

WORDS THAT GO TOGETHER

Write the correct words in the blanks.

alarm clock	goes off	in reality

1. That invention looks silly but _____ it's very useful.

2. My new invention has a bell that _____ when you leave your key in the door.

3. I set my _____ to play music in the morning.

USE

Work with a partner to answer the questions. Use complete sentences.

1. What is something that *floats* on water?

2. How many people can your chair *support*?

3. What color is the *keyboard* you use?

4. What *items* do you usually carry in your pockets or bag?

5. What are some things a *magnet* picks up?

6. What object in your home sits on a *base*?

7. When do you use a *fan*?

8. What size is your computer *screen*?

COMPREHENSION: LONG TALK

UNDERSTANDING THE LISTENING

Listen to the talk. Then circle the letter of the correct answer.

1. The Inventors Club usually _____.
   a. studies past inventions
   b. listens to speakers who are inventors
   c. creates new inventions

2. The woman wants a flying alarm clock because _____.
   a. she usually wakes up late
   b. she likes the sound it makes
   c. she likes things that make her laugh

3. The man knows a lot about _____.
   a. unusual inventions
   b. very important inventions
   c. expensive inventions

REMEMBERING DETAILS

Listen to the talk again. Circle T if the sentence is true. Circle F if the sentence is false.

1. The Inventors Club meets twice a week.	T	F
2. Some unusual inventions are also quite useful.	T	F
3. The flying alarm clock flies around the room until you hit it.	T	F
4. The floating bed uses wires to keep it in the air.	T	F
5. The computer ball has a complete computer inside of it.	T	F
6. There is a necktie that has a pocket to hold a coffee cup.	T	F

TAKING NOTES: Inventions

🎧 *Listen and write notes about the description. Which invention does it describe?*

cell phone   *laptop*

COMPREHENSION: SHORT CONVERSATIONS

🎧 *Listen to the conversations. Then circle the letter of the correct answer.*

CONVERSATION 1

1. Who is the woman talking to?

    a. an inventor in a laboratory

    b. a housekeeper at an agency

    c. a salesperson in a store

2. How does the woman feel?

    a. sleepy

    b. happy

    c. frustrated

CONVERSATION 2

3. What is the woman offering to do for the man?

    a. buy his inventions

    b. talk to the judges at the fair

    c. help get his inventions into another fair

4. How does the man feel?

    a. upset

    b. hopeful

    c. nervous

CONVERSATION 3

5. What does the cell phone in the store have?

    a. a large screen, voice calling, and music

    b. a large screen, video, and music

    c. voice calling, video, and a large screen

6. What kind of salesperson is the man?

    a. rude

    b. helpful

    c. new

DISCUSSION

Discuss the answers to these questions with your classmates.

1. Is a flying alarm clock a good invention? Why or why not?
2. Which invention in the listening do you like best? Why?
3. Do you belong to a club? Why or why not? Why do people like to join clubs? Why are they useful?

CRITICAL THINKING

Work with a partner. Ask each other the following questions. Discuss your answers.

1. What kind of person is an inventor? What personality and characteristics do you think about when you hear the word *inventor*?
2. What new inventions do you think we need in the world today?

LANGUAGE FOCUS

SIMPLE PRESENT WITH ADVERBS OF FREQUENCY

We use the **simple present** to talk about what people do all the time or again and again.

I/You/We/They	**buy** new inventions. **don't (do not) buy** new inventions.
He/She/It	**buys** new inventions. **doesn't (does not) buy** new inventions.

	Adverb of Frequency	
I/You/We/They	**always** **never**	**buy** new inventions. **buy** new inventions.
He/She/It	**always** **never**	**buys** new inventions. **buys** new inventions.

- **Adverbs of frequency** tell us how often something happens.
- Adverbs of frequency come between the subject and the simple present verb, except *be*; adverbs of frequency come after the verb *be*.
- *Always*, *usually*, *often*, *sometimes*, *rarely/seldom*, and *never* are common adverbs of frequency.

0% _____ 100%

| never | rarely/seldom | sometimes | often | usually | always |

*I **always** go to the Tuesday night meetings. They're **often** useful.*

A. *Write a sentence to say how often the person does something. Use the information on the left and the words on the right.*

EXAMPLE: Sally reads a lot, but she has only one book about inventors. (reads/seldom)

Sally seldom reads about inventors.

1. Sam is happy that the library has many books about inventors. (finds/usually)

   _____

2. Hiro has an invention that helps him wake up in time for class. (arrives/always)

   _____

3. Megan has a desktop computer and a laptop, but she likes the laptop better.
    (uses/rarely)

   _____

4. Nate likes to invent things, and a lot of his inventions are useful. (invents/often)

   _____

B. *Work with a partner. Take turns talking about things you and your partner like to do.*

EXAMPLE: I always go for a run on Saturday mornings since I don't have to work.

- always do
- sometimes do
- usually do
- rarely do
- never do

PRONUNCIATION

WORD STRESS: Adverbs of Frequency

A. *Listen to the sentences. Notice the stress on the underlined adverbs of frequency. Then listen again and repeat.*

1. I <u>rarely</u> watch television.
2. He <u>always</u> sends text messages.
3. She <u>never</u> writes letters.
4. I <u>usually</u> turn off my cell phone at night.

B. *Work with a partner. Take turns saying the sentences. Then take turns making and saying new sentences with the adverbs of frequency.*

CONVERSATION

 A. *Listen to the conversation. Then listen again and repeat.*

> **Keith:** What are you doing?
> **Eva:** I'm <u>working on</u> my new invention.
> **Keith:** Well, that <u>sounds boring</u>.
> **Eva:** Actually, I think it's ready to explode!
> **Keith:** Wow! That <u>sounds exciting</u> <u>after all</u>!
> **Eva:** Yes, and it's dangerous, too.

Do you know these expressions? What do you think they mean?

working on	sounds boring	sounds exciting	after all

B. *Work with a partner. Practice a part of the conversation. Replace the underlined words with the words below.*

> **Keith:** What are you doing?
> **Eva:** I'm <u>working on</u> my new invention.

thinking about	making changes to

C. Your Turn. *Write a new conversation. Use some of the words below and your own ideas. Practice the conversation with a partner.*

working on	sounds boring	sounds exciting	after all

 Go to page 142 for the Internet Activity.

DID YOU KNOW?	• In July 2010, Amazon.com reported that for every 100 hardcover books sold over the previous month, 183 Kindle Ebooks had been sold. • The Japanese have a unique word, *chindogu*. It is used for an invention that actually works, but no one would ever use because it would be embarrassing or cause problems.	

WHAT IS BEAUTY AROUND THE WORLD?

before you listen

Answer these questions.

1. What special features do you think make these women beautiful?

2. What special features are considered beautiful or attractive for men or women in your culture?

3. Have ideas about beauty changed over time in a culture that you know? How?

VOCABULARY

MEANING

🎧 *Listen to the talk. Then write the correct words in the blanks.*

complexion	features	ideals	status
elaborate	full	shiny	trendy

1. Teenagers usually wear clothes that are _____ because they want to be popular.

2. Masculine _____ include a strong jaw and chin.

3. Fashion magazines often show people who represent beauty_____ in their culture.

4. Girls like their hair to be healthy and _____.

5. Some cultures think it is beautiful to have a round, _____ body.

6. The type of clothes people wear often show their _____ in society.

7. The natural color of your skin or its condition is your _____.

8. The design of that dress is very _____; it has a lot of colors and patterns.

WORDS THAT GO TOGETHER

Write the correct words in the blanks.

a sign of	inner beauty	pop celebrities

1. Tight, smooth skin is _____ youth.

2. Many young people want to look and act like their culture's _____.

3. Kindness is part of a person's _____.

USE

Work with a partner to answer the questions. Use complete sentences.

1. What is one way to make your hair *shiny*?

2. What is your most attractive facial *feature*?

3. What kind of clothes have *elaborate* designs on them?

4. What is a *trendy* item of clothing that you like?

5. What kind of clothes show a person's *status*?

6. What is the *ideal* of beauty for a man or a woman in your culture?

7. What kind of *complexion* do you have?

8. Who is your favorite *pop celebrity*?

COMPREHENSION: LONG TALK

UNDERSTANDING THE LISTENING

🎧 *Listen to the talk. Then circle the letter of the correct answer.*

1. In _____ culture, ideals of beauty for men and women are different from each other.

   a. American   **b.** African   **c.** Maori

2. The ideal beauty for a Maori always includes having tattoos _____.

   a. on the face only   **b.** with interesting designs   **c.** with simple, square designs

3. The Japanese ideal for masculine beauty is _____.

   a. the same as the American   **b.** having tattoos   **c.** having delicate features

REMEMBERING DETAILS

🎧 *Listen to the talk again. Answer the questions.*

1. Where do men want long stylish hair?
2. Who prefers a strong chin, a square jaw, and a high forehead?
3. What is the beauty ideal for American women?
4. What is a sign of wealth for men in Africa?
5. Where does a Maori man have tattoos?
6. What is a sign of beauty in a Maori woman?

TAKING NOTES: Culture and Beauty

🎧 *Listen and write notes about the description. Which young man does it describe?*

American man

Japanese man

COMPREHENSION: SHORT CONVERSATIONS

🎧 *Listen to the conversations. Then circle the letter of the correct answer.*

CONVERSATION 1

1. What does the hair stylist want to do?
   - **a.** color the woman's hair dark
   - **b.** leave the woman's hair long
   - **c.** color the woman's hair blonde

2. How does the woman feel about cutting her hair?
   - **a.** nervous
   - **b.** sad
   - **c.** excited

CONVERSATION 2

3. Where are the two friends?
   - **a.** at work
   - **b.** at school
   - **c.** at the beach

4. How does the man feel?
   - **a.** excited
   - **b.** shocked
   - **c.** happy

CONVERSATION 3

5. What can the man afford to buy?
   - **a.** the blue shirt
   - **b.** the jeans
   - **c.** the T-shirt

6. What kind of friend is the woman?
   - **a.** generous
   - **b.** unkind
   - **c.** silly

DISCUSSION

Discuss the answers to these questions with your classmates.

1. What are the ideals of beauty for men and women in your culture?
2. Tattoos are very popular for both men and women today. Do you like tattoos? Why or why not?
3. How do pop celebrities influence people's lives today?

CRITICAL THINKING

Work with a partner. Ask each other the following questions. Discuss your answers.

1. Many people get plastic surgery to make them look younger or more like their culture's ideal of beauty. What do you think about plastic surgery? Explain your opinion.

(continued)

2. What does the saying "Beauty is only skin deep" mean? What is the difference between "real" beauty and "ideal" beauty? Do you think that people today are too influenced by the advertising of cosmetic companies? Why or why not?

Language Focus

ORDER OF ADJECTIVES

An **adjective** describes a noun. We sometimes use more than one adjective, but we usually do not use more than three. There are different types of adjectives, such as opinion, size, etc. The usual word order of adjectives is:

1. opinion	2. size	3. age	4. color	5. nationality	6. material

A. *Write the adjectives in the correct order.*

EXAMPLE: black/long/stylish   He has _____*stylish long black*_____ hair.

1. brown/large/lovely   She has _____ eyes.
2. French/new/wool   She has a _____ hat.
3. rosy/young/smooth   The girl has _____ cheeks.
4. purple/large/beautiful   He has a _____ dragon tattooed
   on his arm.
5. red/cotton/old   He loves to wear his _____ shirt.
6. big/white/beautiful   She has _____ teeth.

B. *Work with a partner. Take turns using two or three adjectives to talk about people.*

EXAMPLE: My best friend Luisa is very tall, has brown hair, and loves to wear colorful clothes.
   • a person in your class   • your best friend
   • a person in your family   • your favorite movie star

Pronunciation

WORD STRESS: Adjective + Noun Combinations

A. *Listen to the sentences. Notice the stress on the underlined words. Then listen again and repeat.*

1. <u>American</u> women prefer <u>masculine</u> features with a <u>strong</u> jaw.
2. Americans like <u>white</u> teeth and <u>muscular</u> bodies.
3. The <u>ideal</u> American woman has <u>large</u> eyes and <u>full</u> lips.

4. <u>Japanese</u> girls like boys with <u>long</u> hair and <u>delicate</u> features.

5. Some of their tattoos have <u>beautiful</u> shapes and <u>elaborate</u> patterns.

6. I think <u>inner</u> beauty is <u>more</u> important.

B. *Work with a partner. Take turns saying the sentences.*

CONVERSATION

A. *Listen to the conversation. Then listen again and repeat.*

Audrey: Hey, I like your new denim jacket.

Ryan: Thanks. I like to wear clothes with a <u>trendy look</u>.

Audrey: <u>I see</u>. But you've had the same hairstyle for a long time, right?

Ryan: It's the only thing I won't change.

Audrey: <u>How interesting</u>. I think a shorter cut would look great with your facial features, though.

Ryan: <u>I suppose you're right</u>.

Do you know these expressions? What do you think they mean?

| trendy look | I see | how interesting | I suppose you're right |

B. *Work with a partner. Practice a part of the conversation. Replace the underlined words with the words below.*

Audrey: <u>How interesting</u>. I think a shorter cut would look great with your facial features, though.

Ryan: I suppose you're right.

That's funny.   I understand.

C. Your Turn. *Write a new conversation. Use some of the words below and your own ideas. Practice the conversation with a partner.*

| trendy look | I see | how interesting | I suppose you're right |

Go to page 142 for the Internet Activity.

<table>
<tr><td>**DID YOU KNOW?**</td><td>• It was a common tradition in Vietnam to blacken the teeth of a girl to make her look grown-up and ready for marriage. Many older Vietnamese still have blackened teeth.</td><td></td></tr>
</table>

WHAT COUNTRIES HAVE ROYALTY TODAY?

before you listen

Answer these questions.

1. What countries have kings, queens, or other royalty?

2. How much power do members of royalty have?

3. How do you think members of royalty live?

VOCABULARY

MEANING

🎧 *Listen to the talk. Then write the correct words in the blanks.*

accommodates	astounding	excessive	monarchies
affluent	browsing	fortune	resources

1. I am _____ through a book about the king of Saudi Arabia, and it looks very interesting.

2. It is _____ that some countries still do not allow female royals to be leaders.

3. Some countries have valuable _____, such as gold or oil.

4. The people are angry about the king's _____ spending because the country is poor.

5. Some members of royalty work normal jobs and are not _____ at all.

6. There are ten _____ and twenty-one royal families left in Europe.

7. The king's dining room is very big; it _____ over 200 people.

8. Queen Elizabeth II of England has a personal _____ of about $450 million.

WORDS THAT GO TOGETHER

Write the correct words in the blanks.

estimated value	gold-plated	well off

1. The sultan's yacht is one of the largest and most beautiful in the world, with an _____ of over $700 million.

2. The king of Swaziland is very _____ compared to the people of his country.

3. The royal palace has many amazing things, including _____ dinner plates!

USE

Work with a partner to answer the questions. Use complete sentences.

1. What kind of books or magazines do you *browse* through?
2. Which *monarchies* do you know the most about?
3. What kind of cars do *affluent* people drive?
4. Why does a monarch need a royal palace that *accommodates* hundreds of people?
5. What royal did something that was *astounding* to you?
6. What *resources* does your country have?
7. Who are some people that spend *excessive* amounts of money?
8. How do most royals get their *fortunes*?

COMPREHENSION: LONG TALK

UNDERSTANDING THE LISTENING

Listen to the talk. Then circle the letter of the correct answer.

1. The sultan of Brunei has _____.
   a. complete power
   b. some power
   c. almost no power

2. The sultan lost some of his wealth because _____.
   a. his country's resources ran out
   b. he gave it to the people
   c. he spent it on a wealthy lifestyle

3. The sultan's palace is _____.
   a. the largest that someone lives in
   b. the most expensive in the world
   c. the most luxurious in the world

REMEMBERING DETAILS

Listen to the talk again. Fill in the blanks.

1. Brunei is located on the _____ coast of Borneo.
2. The country makes a fortune from its _____.
3. Most monarchies today don't have much _____.
4. The sultan's _____ has gold-plated furniture.
5. The palace's banquet hall can fit _____ guests.
6. The palace is open only _____ a year.

TAKING NOTES: Royalty

🎧 *Listen and write notes about the description. Which member of royalty does it describe?*

**Queen Elizabeth II
of the United Kingdom**

Queen Rania of Jordan

COMPREHENSION: SHORT CONVERSATIONS

🎧 *Listen to the conversations. Then circle the letter of the correct answer.*

CONVERSATION 1

1. Who is the man talking to?

   a. a friend   **b.** a tour guide   **c.** a member of the royal family

2. How does the man feel about seeing the palace?

   a. confused   **b.** excited   **c.** not interested

CONVERSATION 2

3. Where does the woman live?

   a. the United Kingdom   **b.** the Netherlands   **c.** Denmark

4. How does the man feel about seeing the Queen?

   a. glad   **b.** amazed   **c.** shy

CONVERSATION 3

5. When can the man speak his true feelings?

   a. after he finishes working   **b.** while he is working   **c.** after the woman leaves

6. What is the woman's attitude about the palace?

   a. admiration   **b.** disgust   **c.** boredom

DISCUSSION

Discuss the answers to these questions with your classmates.

1. Do you like the idea of monarchs and royal families in today's world? Why or why not?
2. Why do you think most monarchs today don't have much power? Is this a good or bad thing? Why?
3. Why do you think people love to read about people in royal families, such as Princes Harry and William in the United Kingdom? Are you interested in what royalty are doing? Why or why not?

CRITICAL THINKING

Work with a partner. Ask each other the following questions. Discuss your answers.

1. Is it right for a monarch to become extremely rich because of a country's resources? What else can a monarch do with that money?
2. Do you think spending excessive amounts of money brings happiness? Why or why not? What are the advantages and disadvantages of this lifestyle?

LANGUAGE FOCUS

COMPARATIVE AND SUPERLATIVE ADJECTIVES

We use **comparative adjectives** to compare two people, places, or things.
We use **superlative adjectives** to compare two or more people, places, or things.

Adjective Description	Adjective Example	Comparative	Superlative
short adjectives (1 syllable)	rich young old	richer younger older	the richest the youngest oldest
adjectives ending in *-y*	easy wealthy	easier than wealthier than	the easiest the wealthiest
longer adjectives (2, 3, or 4 syllables)	expensive famous	more expensive than more famous than	the most expensive the most famous
irregular adjectives	good bad little much/many	better than worse than less more	the best the worst the least the most

A. *Look at the information about the monarchs. Write three sentences for each monarch, using the adjectives from the chart on page 18.*

EXAMPLE: King Bhumibol of Thailand

- born: 1927   *King Bhumibol is the oldest monarch.*
- reigned since 1946   *King Bhumibol has reigned longer than Prince Albert II.*
- wealth: US$30 billion   *King Bhumibol is wealthier than both Prince Albert II*
          and Prince Hans Adam.

Prince Albert II of Monaco

- born: 1958   1. _____
- reigned since 2005   2. _____
- wealth: US$1 billion   3. _____

Prince Hans Adam of Lichtenstein

- born: 1946   4. _____
- reigned since 1989   5. _____
- wealth: US$2.5 billion   6. _____

B. *Work with a partner. Take turns talking about people you know using comparatives and superlatives.*

EXAMPLE: There is a woman who lives in my building who is the oldest person I know!

- the oldest   • the youngest   • the best at speaking English
- the funniest   • the most popular   • the most talkative

PRONUNCIATION

WORD STRESS: Superlative Adjectives

A. *Listen to the sentences. Notice the stress on the superlative adjectives. Underline the stressed words. Then listen again and repeat.*

1. He's the most powerful man in his country.
2. It's the oldest castle, you know.
3. He lives in the most luxurious palace.
4. She owns the most valuable diamond.
5. He is the most hardworking monarch.
6. This is by far the most beautiful castle.

B. *Work with a partner. Take turns saying the sentences.*

CONVERSATION

 A. *Listen to the conversation. Then listen again and repeat.*

Announcer:	Congratulations! You have a winning ticket for a tour of Buckingham Palace.
Ilsa:	<u>Are you serious?</u>
Announcer:	Oh, yes. Now, can you go on Monday?
Ilsa:	Oh, no, I can't do that. I have my final exams next week.
Announcer:	<u>What a shame</u>. This ticket is only good for Monday.
Ilsa:	Well, <u>I guess</u> I can give the ticket to my sister. She loves the queen.

Do you know these expressions? What do you think they mean?

Are you serious?   What a shame   I guess

B. *Work with a partner. Practice a part of the conversation. Replace the underlined words with the words below.*

Announcer:	<u>What a shame</u>. This ticket is only good for Monday.
Ilsa:	Well, I guess I can give the ticket to my sister. She loves the queen.

That's too bad.   I'm so sorry.

C. Your Turn. *Write a new conversation. Use some of the words below and your own ideas. Practice the conversation with a partner.*

Are you serious?   What a shame   I guess

 Go to page 143 for the Internet Activity.

DID YOU KNOW?	• In 2008 at age twenty-eight, Jigme Khesar Namgyel Wangchuck of the Himalayan nation of Bhutan became the world's youngest monarch. • The British Royal family changed its last name from Sachsen-Coburg und Gotha to Windsor in 1914. The German name was not appropriate at a time when Britain was at war with Germany.	

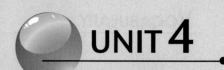

WHAT ARE SOME RITES OF PASSAGE?

before you listen

Answer these questions.

1. What are some times in our lives when big changes take place?

2. What are some ceremonies that mark these times of change?

3. What rites of passage are most important to your family or culture?

VOCABULARY

MEANING

🎧 *Listen to the talk. Then write the correct words in the blanks.*

attach	feat	novice	procession
elastic	leap	occur	ritual

1. I still feel like a(n) _____ at my job, so I need to learn more.
2. Sometimes a group of people walks in a(n) _____ in public during a ceremony or special occasion.
3. Most long stems of trees do not bend or stretch; they aren't _____.
4. Major changes in our relationships usually _____ several times in our lives.
5. One exciting _____ for young people in the United States is their high school graduation ceremony.
6. I want to _____ my cell phone to my bag so I don't lose it.
7. In some rites of passage, individuals must _____ high over things without falling.
8. Sometimes a boy must succeed at a difficult _____ to show he's a man.

WORDS THAT GO TOGETHER

Write the correct words in the blanks.

participate in	take place	take turns

1. Rites of passage _____ in almost every society.
2. Most people _____ some rite of passage during their lives.
3. When you and someone else _____ to do something, you do it one after the other several times.

USE

Work with a partner to answer the questions. Use complete sentences.

1. What is your favorite *ritual* for a birthday?
2. What common everyday task can sometimes be a *feat*?
3. What rituals commonly *occur* during a wedding ceremony?
4. What sport are you a *novice* at?

5. For what occasion in your culture do you see or have a *procession*?

6. What kinds of things do you *attach* to your e-mail to friends or family?

7. What kinds of things do people *leap* over?

COMPREHENSION: LONG TALK

UNDERSTANDING THE LISTENING

Listen to the talk. Then circle the letter of the correct answer.

1. During rites of passage, people _____.
   a. get ready for new responsibilities
   b. enjoy their last days of childhood
   c. compete with others for leadership

2. After their rite of passage, Ethiopian boys _____.
   a. leave their tribe
   b. learn how the men live
   c. have a celebration

3. For boys, most rites of passage to manhood are _____.
   a. not exciting
   b. taken seriously
   c. taken lightly

REMEMBERING DETAILS

Listen to the talk again. Answer the questions.

1. What does a quinceañera celebrate?
2. In land diving, what does a boy attach to his ankles?
3. In Ethiopia, what do boys leap over during their coming-of-age ritual?
4. During Poy Sang Long, who shaves the boy's head?
5. How many days of ceremonies and processions are there during Poy Sang Long?
6. What do the boys put on after they take off their beautiful clothes?

TAKING NOTES: Rites of Passage

Listen and write notes about the description. Which rite of passage does it describe?

high school graduation

quinceañera

COMPREHENSION: SHORT CONVERSATIONS

 Listen to the conversations. Then circle the letter of the correct answer.

CONVERSATION 1

1. Who is the girl talking to?
   a. her father
   b. a guest at her quinceañera
   c. someone at a printing store

2. What is the man's reaction?
   a. disappointment
   b. irritation
   c. fear

CONVERSATION 2

3. What is the young woman going to do?
   a. see her parents
   b. talk to her math teacher
   c. buy a new dress

4. How is the young man feeling?
   a. worried
   b. excited
   c. bored

CONVERSATION 3

5. What does the man want the woman to do?
   a. make decisions about the wedding
   b. change her mind about the wedding
   c. take time to think about the wedding

6. What is the woman's attitude about her wedding?
   a. anger
   b. fear
   c. confusion

DISCUSSION

Discuss the answers to these questions with your classmates.

1. Why are rites for girls and boys different?
2. Why do some boys agree to do dangerous things, such as leap off cliffs during a rite of passage? What do they gain from it?
3. Do you have changes taking place in your life right now? What changes are you looking forward to?

CRITICAL THINKING

Work with a partner. Ask each other the following questions. Discuss your answers.

1. Why are rites of passage important in society? What purpose do they serve? Why do people enjoy their rites of passage?
2. How are rites of passage changing in the modern world, and why are they changing? Is this good or bad? Why?

LANGUAGE FOCUS

BEFORE AND *AFTER* IN TIME CLAUSES

Main Clause	Time Clause
The boy jumps from a tower They enter the monastery	**before** he becomes a man. **after** they participate in ceremonies.
Time Clause	**Main Clause**
Before he becomes a man, **After** they participate in ceremonies,	the boy jumps from a tower. they enter the monastery.

- A **time clause** is a group of words that has a subject and a verb, but it is not a complete sentence.
- A **main clause** is a complete sentence. A time clause needs a main clause to make a complete sentence.
- The main clause can come before or after the time clause. If the time clause comes first, we put a comma after it.

A. *Combine the two sentences to make a new sentence. Be careful. Look at the way each new sentence begins. Add a comma if necessary.*

EXAMPLE: Americans graduate from high school. Americans complete and pass all their classes.

After Americans complete and pass all their classes, they graduate from high school. OR

Before Americans graduate from high school, they complete and pass all their classes. OR

Americans graduate from high school after they complete and pass all their classes. OR

Americans complete and pass all their classes before they graduate from high school.

(continued)

1. You buy a birthday cake. You have a birthday party.

   You buy _____

2. You have a wedding party. You get married.

   You have _____

3. A child is born. You have a religious ceremony.

   After _____

4. You work for a long time. You retire.

   Before _____

B. *Work with a partner. Take turns talking about four things you do before you come to class and four things you do after you come to class. Use* before *and* after.

EXAMPLE: Before I come to class, I read the newspaper.

PRONUNCIATION

VOWEL SOUNDS: *dive* /aɪ/, *wish* /ɪ/, and *leap* /i/

A. *Listen and repeat each word.*

1. dive	rite	vine	time
2. wish	big	fit	him
3. leap	week	free	teen

B. *Listen to the words. Circle the word with the vowel sound that is different.*

1. night	high	like	wish	while
2. heel	sleep	line	tree	creep
3. ring	child	thing	his	wig

CONVERSATION

A. *Listen to the conversation. Then listen again and repeat.*

Natalie: I hear you're turning twenty-one this week. Are you planning a party?

Curtis: As a matter of fact, I am. It's on Saturday night. Would you like to come?

Natalie: I'm supposed to work on Saturday but I'm free after eight o'clock.

Curtis: Good. By the way, I am so glad that I'm not a teenager anymore.

Natalie: Oh, I am, too. I never want to go through those years again.

Curtis: I know those years were hard sometimes, but we had a lot of fun!

Do you know these expressions? What do you think they mean?

as a matter of fact   supposed to   by the way   go through

B. *Work with a partner. Practice a part of the conversation. Replace the underlined words with the words below.*

Natalie: I hear you're turning twenty-one this week. Are you planning a party?

Curtis: <u>As a matter of fact</u>, I am. It's on Saturday night. Would you like to come?

as it turns out   actually

C. Your Turn. *Write a new conversation. Use some of the words below and your own ideas. Practice the conversation with a partner.*

as a matter of fact   supposed to   by the way   go through

Go to page 143 for the Internet Activity.

DID YOU KNOW?

- When an Apache girl was ready to become an adult, she had to go through a four-day ceremony, called the Sun Rise Dance, which included dancing for four days. Today, however, it is reduced to one or two days.
- Modern bungee jumping is similar to land diving on Pentecost Island.

WHO ARE SOME FAMOUS EXPLORERS?

before **you listen**

Answer these questions.

1. What explorers do you know and where did they go?

2. Why do people like to read stories about explorers and their expeditions?

3. Where do you want to explore?

Vocabulary

MEANING

Listen to the talk. Then write the correct words in the blanks.

assignments	challenging	endure	hardships
boundary	encounters	expedition	hostile

1. The explorer's _____ was long, but successful; he went to a rain forest that nobody had ever seen before.

2. Explorers must know what to do if they have _____ with dangerous animals.

3. Explorers sometimes experience _____, like bad weather or not having enough food.

4. Explorers enjoy _____ journeys that test their skill and strength.

5. Unfriendly or _____ people sometimes didn't want explorers coming to their land.

6. He went to explore the wild country, which was the _____ between the two countries.

7. Kings gave men _____ to explore new lands and to do other jobs for their country.

8. Many explorers _____ pain and suffering on their trips, but they keep going because they love the excitement.

WORDS THAT GO TOGETHER

Write the correct words in the blanks.

intrigued by	lost civilizations	were about to

1. The astronauts _____ take a space walk, but first they checked their equipment.

2. Some explorers searched for _____ so they could learn more about an area's history.

3. She was _____ all the interesting animals and plants in the Brazilian rain forest.

USE

Work with a partner to answer the questions. Use complete sentences.

1. What *assignments* do you dislike most in school?
2. What *hardships* do jungle explorers face?
3. When do scientists take *expeditions* to places with ice and snow?
4. What *hostile* environment do you think is more difficult, a hot desert or a frozen land?
5. Where are some *challenging* places for today's explorers?
6. What lost *civilizations* do you know about?
7. What difficulties do travelers *endure* today?
8. Where can travelers have *encounters* with wild animals?

COMPREHENSION: LONG TALK

UNDERSTANDING THE LISTENING

Listen to the talk. Then circle the letter of the correct answer.

1. Fawcett accepted the assignment from the Royal Geographical Society because _____.
   a. the army didn't need him
   b. he loved excitement
   c. he wanted to climb mountains

2. During Fawcett's expeditions in South America _____.
   a. he faced many dangers
   b. he found a hidden city
   c. he helped the local people

3. During Fawcett's last expedition _____.
   a. he starved to death
   b. he was killed by hostile people
   c. he disappeared

REMEMBERING DETAILS

*Listen to the talk again. Circle **T** if the sentence is true. Circle **F** if the sentence is false.*

1. Fawcett was in the British Army for thirty years.   T   F
2. Fawcett explored the boundary between Brazil and Peru.   T   F
3. Hostile people stopped attacking when they heard the music.   T   F
4. A raging river sent Fawcett's boat into a wall of rocks.   T   F
5. On his last expedition, Fawcett went into unexplored land.   T   F
6. Fawcett believed there was a lost city called "Z."   T   F

TAKING NOTES: Continents

🎧 *Listen and write notes about the description. Which continent does it describe?*

Africa

South America

COMPREHENSION: SHORT CONVERSATIONS

🎧 *Listen to the conversations. Then circle the letter of the correct answer.*

CONVERSATION 1

1. Where are the man and woman?

   a. at a library   **b.** at a bookstore   **c.** at a travel agency

2. What is the woman's attitude toward Mary Kingsley?

   a. She admires her.   **b.** She feels sorry for her.   **c.** She doesn't know much about her.

CONVERSATION 2

3. What does the man think he wants to do?

   a. explore the Arctic   **b.** explore the deep sea   **c.** go sailing

4. How is the young man feeling?

   a. worried   **b.** sad   **c.** excited

CONVERSATION 3

5. Where are the man and woman having their conversation?

   a. at the library   **b.** at work   **c.** at a coffee shop

6. What is the man's tone of voice?

   a. unkind   **b.** admiring   **c.** nervous

DISCUSSION

Discuss the answers to these questions with your classmates.

1. Some people said that after Fawcett disappeared, they saw him running through the jungle. Others said he was living as the chief of a tribe. What do you think happened to Percy Fawcett?

2. Why do people make up stories about lost travelers? Why do others love to read about them?

3. The space tourism company, Virgin Galactic, wants to take tourist passengers to the edge of space. Do you want to be one of the first people to take a ride? Why or why not?

CRITICAL THINKING

Work with a partner. Ask each other the following questions. Discuss your answers.

1. Why are explorers and adventurers willing to risk their lives to reach their goal? What characteristics do all explorers and adventurers have in common?

2. Adventure travel is extremely popular today. Why do you think people today want to ride down a raging river, climb mountains, and walk through jungles? Why did people many years ago prefer to travel in comfort? Do you want to take an adventure trip? Why or why not?

LANGUAGE FOCUS

SIMPLE PAST

We use the **simple past** for actions and situations that began and ended in the past.

Statements	Questions and Answers
They **climbed** mountains. They **didn't climb** mountains.	**Q:** **Did** they **climb** mountains? **A:** **Yes,** they **did.** **No,** they **didn't.**
They **went to Brazil**.	**Q:** **Did** they **go** to Brazil? **A:** **Yes,** they **did.** **No,** they **didn't.**

- All subjects use the same verb forms in the simple past.
- We can use specific time expressions such as *yesterday*, *last week*, and *twenty years ago* with the simple past.
- To form the simple past of regular verbs, add *-ed* to the base form. Some verbs are irregular. Their past forms do not end in *-ed*. Some examples are: *become/became*; *go/went*; *fly/flew*.

A. *Complete the paragraph with the simple past of the verbs.*

Jimmy Angel was an American pilot. In 1933, he _____ over an unknown

1. (fly)
area of Venezuela and _____ a huge waterfall. Today, the falls are named after

2. (notice)
him because he _____ them. In 1937, Angel along with four other people

3. (discover)
_____ by plane to the falls. Angel _____ there was gold in this area.

4. (go back) **5. (believe)**
However, his plane got stuck and they could not fly back. The five of them _____

6. (survive)
and _____ for eleven days with little food until they _____ a village.

7. (walk) **8. (reach)**
Jimmy Angel _____ a legend. He _____ in 1956 in a flying accident.

9. (become) **10. (die)**
A model of his plane is at the top of Angel Falls today.

B. *Work with a partner. Take turns asking and answering questions about Jimmy Angel. Use the simple past.*

EXAMPLE: Angel/go/Venezuela?

A: Did Angel go to Venezuela?

B: Yes, he did. He went in 1933.

- Why/falls named after him?
- When/go back/to falls?
- Why/go back/to falls?
- How many days/they/walk?
- What/Angel become?
- How/Angel/die?

PRONUNCIATION

VOWEL SOUNDS: *book* /ʊ/ and *food* /u/

A. *Listen and repeat each word.*

1.	book	cook	pull	wool
2.	food	student	boot	suit

B. *Listen to the words. Check the box for the vowel sound you hear.*

	book /ʊ/	food /u/
1. soon		
2. too		
3. look		
4. moon		
5. good		
6. two		
7. pool		
8. fool		

CONVERSATION

A. *Listen to the conversation. Then listen again and repeat.*

Alex: Are you joining Lisa on her summer trip?

Cindy: I wanted to, but it <u>took her ages</u> to make the arrangements. <u>After a while</u>, I made other plans.

Alex: I wanted to go, too. But a friend just <u>offered me a job</u> as his assistant.

Cindy: That's great. Anyway, now I'm going on a ten-day hike to visit some ancient sites in Egypt.

Alex: That sounds challenging. But be careful. I've <u>heard stories about</u> poisonous snakes and mysterious deaths.

Cindy: Very funny. Anyway, you can't scare me so easily.

Do you know these expressions? What do you think they mean?

took ages   after a while   offer someone a job   hear stories about

B. *Work with a partner. Practice a part of the conversation. Replace the underlined words with the words below.*

Alex: I wanted to go, too. But a relative just <u>offered me a job</u> as his assistant.

Cindy: That's great. Anyway, now I'm going on a ten-day hike to visit some ancient sites in Egypt.

asked me to work   gave me a position

C. Your Turn. *Write a new conversation. Use some of the words below and your own ideas. Practice the conversation with a partner.*

took ages   after a while   offer someone a job   hear stories about

 *Go to page 144 for the Internet Activity.*

<table>
<tr><td>

**DID
YOU
KNOW?**

</td><td>

- In 1778, Captain Cook was the first European to discover Hawaii. On his first trip, the Hawaiians were very nice to him, but when he returned in 1779, they killed him.
- Marco Polo was an Italian explorer who traveled throughout Europe and Asia between 1260 and 1295. When he returned, he wrote a book about what he saw. People called it *Il Milione*, or a book of a million lies, because many people didn't believe his stories.

</td><td>

</td></tr>
</table>

UNIT 6

WHAT ARE SOME JOBS THAT ARE UNIQUE TO AUSTRALIA?

before **you listen**

Answer these questions.

1. Some jobs, such as flying doctor, sheep shearer, snake catcher, and crocodile hunter are unique to Australia. Why do you think this is?

2. What are some unusual jobs in your country?

3. What are some dangerous jobs in your country?

VOCABULARY

MEANING

Listen to the talk. Then write the correct words in the blanks.

allow	capture	harbor	mean
bait	endangered	jaws	trained

1. The officers are careful not to hurt the animals when they _____ them.
2. I enjoy walking near the _____ because I like to look at the boats and the water.
3. They tried a new _____ when they went fishing, and they caught a lot more fish.
4. My sister is a(n) _____ actress and she is going to be in a play in the new town theater.
5. It's a good idea to stay away from animals with big _____. They could be dangerous.
6. My school doesn't _____ students to have their cell phones on in class.
7. Sometimes, schoolchildren are _____ to a new student, so the teachers should tell them to be nice.
8. We should try and protect _____ animals and plants because it keeps the world healthy and balanced.

WORDS THAT GO TOGETHER

Write the correct words in the blanks.

go for it	rely on	set a trap

1. When people or rangers want to catch a wild animal, they _____ for it.
2. People trust and _____ the rangers to help them, especially if they are having a problem.
3. When a hungry wild animal sees food, it will always _____.

USE

Work with a partner to answer the questions. Use complete sentences.

1. What animal has big *jaws*?
2. Why don't parents *allow* children to touch some animals?

(continued on next page)

3. What are some animals that are *mean* when people get in their way?

4. What are two *endangered* animals?

5. What purpose does a *harbor* serve?

6. What kind of *bait* is good to catch a mouse?

7. When is it sometimes necessary to *capture* an animal?

8. What is a job that you must be *trained* to do?

COMPREHENSION: LONG TALK

UNDERSTANDING THE LISTENING

🎧 *Listen to the talk. Then circle the letter of the correct answer.*

1. The government stopped people from hunting crocodiles because _____.
   a. it was too dangerous for people
   b. people killed too many crocodiles
   c. the Parks and Wildlife Service needed jobs

2. Parks officers trap crocodiles in Darwin Harbor because _____.
   a. the crocodiles are a danger to people
   b. the crocodile farms need them
   c. there aren't enough crocodiles in the territory

3. Officers catch a crocodile by _____.
   a. making a trap for it
   b. hitting it with a boat
   c. tying it to the back of the boat

REMEMBERING DETAILS

🎧 *Listen to the talk again. Fill in the blanks.*

1. In the Northern Territory, there are around _____ crocodiles.

2. In the last thirty years, crocodiles have killed ten people and injured around _____.

3. People _____ in Darwin Harbor even though there are crocodiles.

4. There are not enough trained _____ to capture all the crocodiles in the harbor.

5. The officers tie the crocodile's _____ together before they pull it in the boat.

6. The man lost two _____ when he was tying a crocodile's jaws.

TAKING NOTES: Animals

🎧 *Listen and write notes about the description. Which Australian animal does it describe?*

kangaroo

koala

COMPREHENSION: SHORT CONVERSATIONS

🎧 *Listen to the conversations. Then circle the letter of the correct answer.*

CONVERSATION 1

1. What bait does the store have?

   a. worms   **b.** flies   **c.** eggs

2. How does the man feel?

   a. fascinated   **b.** tired   **c.** eager

CONVERSATION 2

3. What does the woman want to do?

   a. work in sales   **b.** be a snake catcher   **c.** be a crocodile hunter

4. What is the man's attitude toward the woman?

   a. disappointment   **b.** disbelief   **c.** happiness

CONVERSATION 3

5. Why didn't the woman go to Sydney?

   a. She didn't have a tour guide.   **b.** She was too ill.   **c.** The group canceled the trip.

6. How does the woman feel about her trip?

   a. disappointed   **b.** grateful   **c.** nervous

DISCUSSION

Discuss the answers to these questions with your classmates.

1. Would you like to work with animals? Why or why not? What career do you want and why?
2. What personality traits and skills do people need to do dangerous jobs?
3. Why do some people choose unusual or dangerous jobs that few other people want to do?

CRITICAL THINKING

Work with a partner. Ask each other the following questions. Discuss your answers.

1. Landowners in the Northern Territory want to kill the crocodiles. Why do you think they want to do that? Should the government of Australia allow them to kill the crocodiles? Why or why not?
2. In areas around the world, the problem of wild animals coming near humans is getting worse. Tigers kill people in India. Elephants ruin crops in Africa. Bears play in swimming pools in the United States. What do you think is causing this problem? How can we solve it?

LANGUAGE FOCUS

THE CONDITIONAL WITH THE PRESENT AND THE PAST

We use the **conditional** to talk about situations that are not true at the moment.

If Clause (Present)	Main Clause (*will/won't*)
If we **capture** all the crocodiles,	we **will be** safe.
Main Clause (*will/won't*)	***If* Clause (Present)**
We **will be** safe	if we **capture** all the crocodiles

If Clause (Past)	Main Clause (*would/wouldn't have*)
If we **had hired** more catchers,	we **would have captured** more crocodiles.
Main Clause (*would/wouldn't*)	***If* Clause (Past)**
We **would have captured** more crocodiles	if we **had hired** more catchers.

- Conditional sentences often use *if* clauses. An *if* clause alone is not a complete sentence. An *if* clause and a main clause make a complete sentence.

- In the present, the *if* clause can come before or after the main clause with no difference in meaning. If the *if* clause comes first, we put a comma after it.
- In the past, the *if* clause can also come before or after the main clause with no difference in meaning. We use the past perfect in the *if* clause and *would (not) have* + past participle in the main clause. If the *if* clause comes first, we put a comma after it.

A. *Complete the sentences with the correct word and form of the verb. Use a comma where necessary.*

EXAMPLE: If you go to a zoo, (you / see) _____you will see_____ many interesting animals.

1. If you set a trap, (you / catch) _____ a crocodile.
2. The (crocodile / go) _____ to the trap if it is hungry.
3. A trap door will come down if a (crocodile / pull) _____ on the meat.
4. It will be safe if (we / tie) _____ the crocodile's jaws.
5. If they hadn't hunted crocodiles (they / not be) _____ endangered.
6. They would have seen more crocodiles if (they / go) _____ to the nature preserve in good weather.

B. *Work with a partner. Take turns asking and answering questions using "What would you do if . . ." and the information below.*

EXAMPLE: . . . your friend wanted to be a crocodile hunter

A: What would you do if your friend wanted to be a crocodile hunter?

B: If my friend wanted to be a crocodile hunter, I would tell him that that job is too dangerous!

- someone wanted you to come on a trip to Australia
- you went to the outback in Australia
- you saw a crocodile
- someone gave you a pet snake

PRONUNCIATION

-ER AND -OR ENDINGS

A. *Listen to the words. Notice the -er and -or endings. Do they sound the same or different? Then listen again and repeat.*

teacher   doctor

B. *Write -er or -or in the blanks. Use a dictionary if you need help. Then listen and repeat the sentences.*

1. He's a crocodile hunt___.
2. He's a trained offic___.
3. We went to Darwin Harb___.

4. Do you want to be a snake catch___?
5. I want to be a cattle ranch___.
6. She is a park rang___.

CONVERSATION

 A. *Listen to the conversation. Then listen again and repeat.*

Linda: Guess what? I got a job in the outback in Australia.

Julio: Wow, that's great. <u>Then again</u>, it's very isolated.

Linda: Yes, it's miles from civilization. I almost said no, but then I decided to <u>go for it</u>.

Julio: But there are no stores, no schools, no hospitals.

Linda: <u>That's true</u>. But I can ride horses and experience a whole new way of life.

Julio: Yes, and work like a fool for very little pay. Well, you won't catch me going with you, <u>believe me</u>.

Do you know these expressions? What do you think they mean?

then again   **go for it**   **that's true**   **believe me**

B. *Work with a partner. Practice a part of the conversation. Replace the underlined words with the words below.*

Linda: Guess what? I got a job in the outback in Australia.

Julio: Wow, that's great. <u>Then again</u>, it's very isolated.

on the other hand   **but the fact is**

C. Your Turn. *Write a new conversation. Use some of the words below and your own ideas. Practice the conversation with a partner.*

then again   **go for it**   **that's true**   **believe me**

Go to page 144 for the Internet Activity.

DID YOU KNOW?	• The largest cattle station in Australia is the same size as Belgium.	

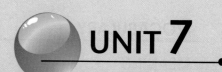

WHAT HAVE THE CHINESE GIVEN THE WORLD?

you listen

before

Answer these questions.

1. What are some things that China is famous for?
2. What is a famous invention from your culture?
3. What are some things that you like or use that originate from different cultures?

Vocabulary

MEANING

🎧 *Listen to the talk. Then write the correct words in the blanks.*

appetizing	exquisite	mentioned	originated
compass	handy	order	tomb

1. Things like matches and paper money are very _____, or useful, items.

2. We were hungry when we got to the restaurant and wanted to _____ our food right away.

3. Many cultures place dead bodies inside a(n) _____.

4. All the cakes and cookies look so _____. I want to eat all of them!

5. The teacher _____ that final grades would be given out next week.

6. I always bring a(n) _____ when I take a long walk in the woods so I don't get lost.

7. That silk dress is _____. It's the most beautiful dress I have ever seen.

8. Pasta _____ in China, but many countries make something similar, too.

WORDS THAT GO TOGETHER

Write the correct words in the blanks.

be famished	had a clue	lose one's way

1. These street signs are so confusing that it's easy to _____.

2. You haven't eaten all day, so you must _____.

3. That's new to me. I never _____ that the Chinese invented pasta.

USE

Work with a partner to answer the questions. Use complete sentences.

1. What is something *handy* that you use every day?

2. What is the most *appetizing* food you ate yesterday?

3. What is the most *exquisite* thing you own?

4. Where do you think tea *originated* from?

5. What is a food you like to *order* in a restaurant?

6. Where is a place in which you sometimes *lose your way*?

7. What is a word or phrase that makes you feel happy when a person *mentions* it?

8. When is a *compass* useful?

COMPREHENSION: LONG TALK

UNDERSTANDING THE LISTENING

🎧 *Listen to the talk. Then circle the letter of the correct answer.*

1. The Chinese have invented _____.
   a. only things related to food
   b. more things than the Italians
   c. things that are both useful and beautiful

2. Chinese paper money was called "flying money" because _____.
   a. it wasn't worth very much
   b. it was easy to spend all of it
   c. it was made of thin paper

3. We know that the Chinese used a compass in the third century because _____.
   a. someone wrote about it
   b. researchers discovered one in a tomb
   c. a person found one while searching for valuable stones

REMEMBERING DETAILS

🎧 *Listen to the talk again. Fill in the blanks.*

1. Some people think the Italians invented _____, but the Chinese did.

2. Another food the Chinese invented is _____.

3. The Chinese invented the wheelbarrow around the _____ century B.C.E.

4. Chinese paper money was very _____, so it could blow away easily.

5. Someone found the world's oldest _____ in a tomb.

6. People used a compass so they wouldn't get _____.

TAKING NOTES: Inventions

 Listen and write notes about the description. Which invention does it describe?

fireworks

cannon

COMPREHENSION: SHORT CONVERSATIONS

Listen to the conversations. Then circle the letter of the correct answer.

CONVERSATION 1

1. What did the woman buy?

   a. a ring   **b.** a hat   **c.** a pair of gloves

2. How is the man feeling?

   a. irritated   **b.** confused   **c.** proud

CONVERSATION 2

3. What does the man want to do?

   a. see the palace   **b.** stay at the hotel   **c.** walk around Beijing

4. How does the man feel?

   a. upset   **b.** happy   **c.** tired

CONVERSATION 3

5. What does the man want the woman to do?

   a. take a walk   **b.** buy the kite   **c.** have a rest

6. How does the man feel?

   a. tired   **b.** relieved   **c.** nervous

DISCUSSION

Discuss the answers to these questions with your classmates.

1. What do you think is the most important invention that originated in China? Why?
2. China officially used paper money in the tenth century. Sweden used the first Western paper money in 1661. Why did all countries eventually use paper money? What are the advantages of paper money? What are the disadvantages?
3. Do you get lost easily or are you good at directions? How did people find their way before the invention of the compass? What new inventions help people find their way?

CRITICAL THINKING

Work with a partner. Ask each other the following questions. Discuss your answers.

1. Think of your three favorite things? Are they beautiful? Useful? Both?
2. Countries make a great effort to prove that they invented certain things. Why is it so important to countries to claim their inventions? Do you think people do the same thing? Why?

LANGUAGE FOCUS

SIMPLE PAST (REVIEW) AND PRESENT PERFECT

Simple Past	Present Perfect
Use for actions that began and ended in the past.	Use for actions that began in the past, continue to the present, and may continue into the future.
Use to talk about a definite time in the past, for example, *yesterday, ten days ago, 500 years ago.*	Use to talk about indefinite time up to the present, for example, *ever, never, recently, today, this week* when these periods of time are not finished.
I **lived** in China last year.	She **has lived** in China for two years.

- We form the **present perfect** with *have* + the past participle.
- We often use the **present perfect** with *for* or *since* to talk about length of time.
- We use *for* to talk about length of time. We use *since* to talk about when a period of time began.

I have known him **for** *a year. I have known him* **since** *2009.*

(continued)

Present Perfect: Questions	Present Perfect: Statements
Have I/we/you/they **eaten** it?	I/We/You/They**'ve (have) eaten** it. I/We/You/They **haven't (have not) eaten** it.
Has he/she/it **eaten** it?	He/She/It**'s (has) eaten** it. He/She/It **hasn't (has not) eaten** it.
How long have I/we/you/they **known** Lin?	I/We/You/They**'ve (have) known** Lin for a year. I/We/You/They **haven't (have not) known** Lin for too long.
How long has he/she/it **known** Lin?	He/She/It**'s (has) known** Lin since 2005. He/She/It **hasn't (has not) known** Lin for too long.

A. *Complete the sentences with the simple past or present perfect of the verbs.*

1. The Chinese (invent) _____ paper over 2,000 years ago.
2. I (eat) _____ Chinese food three times this week.
3. She (wear) _____ a beautiful silk dress last night.
4. I never (see) _____ a Chinese kite.
5. She (visit) _____ China many times.
6. They (find) _____ another tomb in China recently.

B. *Work with a partner. Take turns asking and answering questions using* have you *and the information below.*

EXAMPLE:

A: Have you been to China?

B: Yes, I have. OR No, I haven't.

- eaten with chopsticks
- heard about the Forbidden City
- used firecrackers
- flown a kite

PRONUNCIATION

REDUCED FORM OF *FOR*

A. *Listen to the sentences. Notice the reduced pronunciation of* for. *Listen again and repeat.*

1. He's lived here for ten years.
2. She's studied English for three years.
3. We've waited for many weeks.
4. I've been here for twenty-five minutes.
5. They've been here for a long time.
6. It's been cold for two days.

B. *Work with a partner. Take turns asking and answering the questions below. Use the reduced form of* for.

1. How long have you lived here?
2. How long have you studied English?
3. How long have you been in this classroom today?

CONVERSATION

A. *Listen to the conversation. Then listen again and repeat.*

Brandon: I was famished, so I just ate three bowls of Chinese noodles.

Lisa: Wow, that's a lot of noodles! <u>By the way</u>, is the library open today?

Brandon: I <u>don't have a clue</u>. Why do you ask?

Lisa: I'm writing a paper on inventions from India, and I need more information.

Brandon: Why don't you just <u>take it easy</u> today? You're always working too hard.

Lisa: Well, that's easy for you to say, <u>isn't it</u>? You finished your paper last week!

Do you know these expressions? What do you think they mean?

> by the way   don't have a clue   take it easy   isn't it

B. *Work with a partner. Practice a part of the conversation. Replace the underlined words with the words below.*

Brandon: I <u>don't have a clue</u>. Why do you ask?

Lisa: I'm writing a paper on inventions from India, and I need more information.

> don't have any idea   couldn't tell you

C. Your Turn. *Write a new conversation. Use some of the words below and your own ideas. Practice the conversation with a partner.*

> by the way   don't have a clue   take it easy   isn't it

Go to page 145 for the Internet Activity.

DID YOU KNOW?

- The Chinese invented the world's first written exams in the seventh century. They were for people who wanted to be officials of the state. The exams lasted seventy-two hours.

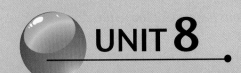

WHO ARE SOME FAMOUS SCIENTISTS IN MEDICINE?

before you listen

Answer these questions.

1. What are some famous medical discoveries?

2. What illnesses do we still not have cures for?

3. How do you think people cured basic health problems, such as a headache or stomachache, in the past?

VOCABULARY

MEANING

🎧 *Listen to the talk. Then write the correct words in the blanks.*

astonished	conduct	infected	spots
brilliant	cure	odd	trials

1. Researchers have to do _____ to see how a new medicine works and to make sure it is safe.

2. Sadly, many diseases do not have a _____, so scientists must keep looking.

3. The _____ young student knew more about the experiment than her professor did!

4. The doctor was _____ that his patient got better. She was very sick, and he thought she was going to die.

5. Scientists have to _____ tests to see if a new medicine works.

6. The new doctor had _____ ideas about how to treat the disease, but they worked, and the patient got better.

7. A wound that is badly _____ can spread disease throughout the body.

8. The dark _____ on his skin are unusual, but they are not dangerous.

WORDS THAT GO TOGETHER

Write the correct words in the blanks.

by accident	float away	land on

1. Some things are so small and light that they can easily _____ into the air.

2. I put salt in my coffee _____; it tasted terrible!

3. Be careful walking on the ice. You don't want to fall and _____ your back!

USE

Work with a partner to answer the questions. Use complete sentences.

1. Who do you think was or is a *brilliant* scientist?

2. What kinds of things can a person *conduct*?

(continued)

3. What news *astonished* you recently?

4. What do you want scientists to find a *cure* for?

5. What can cause you to have *spots* on your skin?

6. How do you stop a cut from getting *infected*?

7. What *odd* things are interesting to you?

8. What is something you did *by accident* recently?

COMPREHENSION: LONG TALK

UNDERSTANDING THE LISTENING

Listen to the talk. Then circle the letter of the correct answer.

1. Alexander Fleming wanted to develop a cure for infections because _____.
   a. he wanted to win the Nobel Prize
   b. he wanted to help soldiers
   c. he wanted to cure his brother

2. Fleming discovered penicillin by _____.
   a. reading about it in a journal
   b. finding it on a plate of bacteria
   c. finding it in another scientist's laboratory

3. Fleming stopped his experiments on penicillin because _____.
   a. he couldn't produce it the right way
   b. he wanted to be a chemist
   c. he couldn't see any use for it

REMEMBERING DETAILS

Listen to the talk again. Answer the questions.

1. In what war was Fleming a doctor in the British army?

2. What was Fleming growing during his experiment in 1928?

3. Where did the other scientist's mold go?

4. What did the mold do to the bacteria next to it?

5. What did Chain and Florey do after they read Fleming's article?

6. What did the scientists receive in 1945?

TAKING NOTES: Treatments

🎧 *Listen and write notes about the description. Which treatment does it describe?*

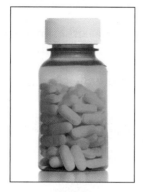

aspirin

Vitamin C

COMPREHENSION: SHORT CONVERSATIONS

🎧 *Listen to the conversations. Then circle the letter of the correct answer.*

CONVERSATION 1

1. Where are the speakers?

   a. at home   **b.** at a shop   **c.** at a restaurant

2. How is the woman feeling?

   a. upset   **b.** satisfied   **c.** proud

CONVERSATION 2

3. Who is the man talking to?

   a. his professor   **b.** a scientist   **c.** a student

4. What is the woman's tone of voice?

   a. unkind   **b.** admiring   **c.** bored

CONVERSATION 3

5. What did the man do about his cut?

   a. He went to the hospital.   **b.** He put medicine on it.   **c.** He saw his doctor.

6. What is the woman feeling?

   a. annoyance   **b.** happiness   **c.** concern

DISCUSSION

Discuss the answers to these questions with your classmates.

1. Why was the invention of penicillin so important? What other medical discoveries had a great influence on our health?
2. What did people do to cure themselves of illness before they had the drugs available today?
3. What personality and character traits do you think a research scientist has? What do research scientists contribute to society?

CRITICAL THINKING

Work with a partner. Ask each other the following questions. Discuss your answers.

1. What are some dangers of taking certain kinds of medicine?
2. There are drugs that can easily save lives, but they don't get to many people who need them. Who are some of these people? Why aren't they getting the medicine they need? What can we do about it?

LANGUAGE FOCUS

SIMPLE PAST (REVIEW) AND PAST PROGRESSIVE

Simple Past	Past Progressive
Use for actions that began and ended in the past.	Use for actions in progress at a certain time in the past.
He **grew** bacteria. Many soldiers **died**.	One day, he **was growing** bacteria on a plate. During the war, many soldiers **were dying** from infected wounds.

- We form the **past progressive** with the past tense of *be* and the base form of a verb + *-ing*.
- We can use the **simple past** and the **past progressive** in the same sentence.
- When one action interrupts another action, we use *while* before the past progressive action or *when* before the simple past action. The sentences below have the same meaning.

> **While** he **was growing** bacteria, he **noticed** something.
> He **was growing** bacteria **when** he **noticed** something.

- We can change the order of the sentence with *when* or *while*. When we begin a sentence with a clause using *when* or *while*, we put a comma after the clause.

A. *Complete the sentences with the simple past or past progressive of the verbs.*

1. Alexander Fleming (grow) _____ bacteria when he discovered penicillin.

2. Fleming (study) _____ a rare mold when the spores of the mold flew away.

3. When Fleming (return) _____ from vacation, he looked at the plate of bacteria.

4. Alexander Graham Bell (do) _____ an experiment when he had an accident.

5. While Thomas Watson (work) _____ on another floor, he heard Bell's voice on the telephone.

6. When Watson (hear) _____, "Mr. Watson, come here. I want you," he ran to Bell's room. People say this was the world's first telephone call.

B. *Work with a partner. Take turns asking and answering questions about what was happening. Use the information below.*

EXAMPLE:

A: What were doing when you received your last text message?

B: I was sitting on a bus when I received my last text message

- What were you wearing when you came to class today?
- What was happening when you saw your friends recently?
- What were you feeling when you went home yesterday?
- What were you doing when you felt tired last night?

PRONUNCIATION

IS/ARE AND WAS/WERE

 A. *Listen and circle the letter of the sentence you hear.*

1. **a.** It was raining.
   b. It's raining.

2. **a.** He was studying.
   b. He's studying.

3. **a.** She was working.
   b. She's working.

4. **a.** What were you feeling?
   b. What are you feeling?

5. **a.** What were they doing?
   b. What are they doing?

6. **a.** We were sleeping.
   b. We are sleeping.

B. *Work with a partner. Take turns saying the sentences.*

CONVERSATION

 A. *Listen to the conversation. Then listen again and repeat.*

Haley: Did you find the letter you were looking for?

Jake: Yes, I found it by accident in my medical book. I <u>have no idea</u> how it got there.

Haley: If you <u>paid attention</u> to what you were doing, you wouldn't lose things all the time.

Jake: I know. I'm always <u>in a hurry</u> and then I forget where I put things.

Haley: Well, just be more careful from now on.

Jake: You're right. Now, <u>by any chance</u>, did you see my car keys?

Do you know these expressions? What do you think they mean?

| have no idea | paid attention | in a hurry | by any chance |

B. *Work with a partner. Practice a part of the conversation. Replace the underlined words with the words below.*

Haley: If you <u>paid attention to</u> what you were doing, you wouldn't lose things all the time.

Jake: I know. I'm always in a hurry and then I forget where I put things.

thought about   showed some interest in

C. Your Turn. *Write a new conversation. Use some of the words below and your own ideas. Practice the conversation with a partner.*

have no idea   paid attention   in a hurry   by any chance

 Go to page 145 for the Internet Activity.

DID YOU KNOW?

- Patients stayed awake during operations until 1846, when an American dentist, William Morton, used ether as an anesthetic on a patient.
- Eyeglasses were invented in the late thirteenth century. But it took inventors 400 more years to add the sidepieces that keep them in place.
- In 1667, doctors gave a patient a blood transfusion using the blood of a lamb. The patient survived!

WHO ARE SOME FAMOUS DETECTIVE STORY CHARACTERS?

you listen

before

Answer these questions.

1. Why do people hire detectives?
2. Do you read mystery books? If so, which is your favorite? If not, why not?
3. Who are some detective characters that you know? What do like or dislike about the characters?

VOCABULARY

MEANING

 *Listen to the talk. Then write the correct words in the blanks.*

character	chasing	intuition	solve
charming	eventually	mysterious	van

1. I usually have good _____ when I meet people, even when I don't know a lot about them.

2. The police were _____ the criminal for twenty minutes, and they finally caught him!

3. The mother was my favorite _____ in that movie because she was very smart and funny.

4. A detective who can _____ cases knows how to find answers and information about crimes.

5. Lin lives in New York now, but _____ she wants to move back to Beijing.

6. Jim has a lot of friends because he is so sweet and _____.

7. His sudden death was _____ because he was young and very healthy.

8. Joe is going to help Lena move because he has a big _____ that can fit a lot of her furniture and boxes.

WORDS THAT GO TOGETHER

Write the correct words in the blanks.

came up with	formal training	private detective

1. The author _____ the character of Precious in *The No. 1 Ladies' Detective Agency* when he was in Botswana.

2. The _____ helped Ray find out that his business partner was stealing money from him.

3. Rajika got a new job at the bank, so she will have one month of _____ at the main office.

USE

Work with a partner to answer the questions. Use complete sentences.

1. How does a *charming* person act?
2. Who do you know who has good *intuition*?
3. Who is your favorite *character* from books or movies?
4. What kinds of cases does your favorite TV detective *solve*?
5. Who is a famous *private detective* from books or television?
6. Why is a *van* a good car for a small business?
7. What job do you *eventually* want to have?
8. Where do *mysterious* things sometimes happen?

COMPREHENSION: LONG TALK

UNDERSTANDING THE LISTENING

Listen to the talk. Then circle the letter of the correct answer.

1. Precious Ramotswe is different from other detectives because _____.

   a. she's a mysterious character
   b. she lives in a big city and solves major crimes
   c. she's a sweet woman living in a small African town

2. Precious is a good detective because _____.

   a. she has a lot of training
   b. she knows a lot about people
   c. she has the best equipment

3. McCall Smith got the idea for his first story about Precious Ramotswe because _____.

   a. he knew someone like her
   b. he read a story about a charming woman
   c. he saw a woman who looked interesting

REMEMBERING DETAILS

*Listen to the talk again. Circle **T** if the sentence is true. Circle **F** if the sentence is false.*

1. People call Precious Ramotswe the Miss Marple of Botswana.   T   F

2. Precious has her business in a very modern office.   T   F

3. Precious is Botswana's only formally trained private detective.   T   F

4. Precious is a very stern and serious woman.   T   F

5. McCall Smith was born in Zimbabwe.   T   F

6. Smith wrote short stories about Precious before he wrote the novels.   T   F

TAKING NOTES: Detective Story Characters

Listen and write notes about the description. Which detective character does it describe?

Sherlock Holmes

James Bond

COMPREHENSION: SHORT CONVERSATIONS

Listen to the conversations. Then circle the letter of the correct answer.

CONVERSATION 1

1. Who is the man speaking to?

   a. his wife   **b.** the owner of the house   **c.** a real estate agent

2. What is the woman's attitude about the house?

   a. She likes it.   **b.** She thinks it's mysterious.   **c.** She doesn't want the man to see it.

CONVERSATION 2

3. What does the woman want the man to do?

   a. solve a murder   **b.** stop a robbery   **c.** find someone who is following her

4. How is the woman feeling?

   a. confident   **b.** tired   **c.** afraid

(continued)

5. What does the woman want to be?

    a. a chef   **b.** a nurse   **c.** a private detective

6. How does the man feel?

    a. frustrated   **b.** nervous   **c.** sad

DISCUSSION

Discuss the answers to these questions with your classmates.

1. Why is intuition a good thing to have in life? When do we use it? Why do we often rely on it?

2. What is the most mysterious thing that has ever happened to you? Why do people love a good mystery?

3. What characteristics are good to have if you want to be a private detective?

CRITICAL THINKING

Work with a partner. Ask each other the following questions. Discuss your answers.

1. Whom do you think makes a better detective, a man or a woman. Why? What kind of cases would a woman be better at solving? What kind of cases would a man be better at solving? Why?

2. Precious solves everyday problems for her customers and lives in a small African town. This is unusual for detective stories, so some people think it is surprising that *The No. 1 Ladies' Detective Agency* is so popular. Do you agree? Why or why not?

LANGUAGE FOCUS

ADJECTIVE CLAUSES WITH *WHO*, *WHOM*, AND *THAT* REFERRING TO PEOPLE

An **adjective clause** gives information about a noun in the main clause.

Main Clause	Adjective Clause
A detective is a person	**that** finds out about people.
There is the detective	**who** solved the crime.
That's the detective	**whom** I talked to.

- *Who* and *that* are relative pronouns. They begin adjective clauses.
- *Who* and *that* refer to people. Both are correct, but *who* is usually preferred for people.
- *Who* and *that* are usually subjects of an adjective clause.
- *Whom* refers to people also. *Whom* is always the object of an adjective clause. *Note: Whom* is used in formal English, such as when giving a speech or in writing in school. In everyday English, we use *that* or *who* as an object relative pronoun.

A. *Write questions and answers using the statements. Combine the sentences into one sentence. Use* who *for a subject and* whom *for an object.*

EXAMPLE: Hercule Poirot was a detective. This detective solved many crimes.

A: Who was Hercule Poirot?

B: Hercule Poirot was a detective who solved crimes.

1. Miss Marple was an elderly woman. This woman solved many crimes.

   _____

2. That man is an actor. I saw him in a movie last week.

   _____

3. Hercule Poirot and Miss Marple are detectives. These detectives appear in many of Agatha Christie's stories.

   _____

4. Ian Fleming is a writer. He created the character of James Bond.

   _____

5. Peter Sellers was an actor. This actor played Inspector Clouseau.

   _____

6. Peter Sellers was an actor. I think he was very funny.

   _____

B. *Work with a partner. Take turns asking and answering six questions about what a person does. Use* who *or* what.

EXAMPLE:

A: What do we call a person who investigates crimes?

B: A detective.

PRONUNCIATION

PLURAL ENDINGS: *desks* /s/, *stories* /z/, and *watches* /ɪz/

A. *Listen to the plural endings of the underlined words. Then listen again and repeat.*

1. They sit at their <u>desks</u>.
2. They tell a lot of <u>stories</u>.
3. They looked at their <u>watches</u>.

B. *Listen to the sentences. Check the box for the plural ending you hear.*

	desks /s/	stories /z/	watches /ɪz/
1. Her office has <u>books</u>.			
2. He speaks several <u>languages</u>.			
3. She wrote many <u>novels</u>.			
4. She also wrote <u>plays</u>.			
5. He has many <u>boxes</u>.			
6. On her table, there are <u>teacups</u>.			

CONVERSATION

A. *Listen to the conversation. Then listen again and repeat.*

Don: No one's here. Where is everyone?

Wanda: That's no mystery. There's a sale at the bookstore. Things are <u>flying off the shelves</u>.

Don: Oh, that's right. <u>Anyway</u>, I need someone who can help me practice my French.

Wanda: Well, <u>you're in luck</u> because I can do that.

Don: You speak French?

Wanda: Sure. I lived in France for a year. <u>The rest is history</u>.

Do you know these expressions? What do you think they mean?

flying off the shelves   anyway   you're in luck   the rest is history

B. *Work with a partner. Practice a part of the conversation. Replace the underlined words with the words below.*

Don: You speak French?

Wanda: Sure. I lived in France for a year. <u>The rest is history</u>.

| Everyone knows what happened next | That had an important effect on the rest of my life |

C. Your Turn. *Write a new conversation. Use some of the words below and your own ideas. Practice the conversation with a partner.*

flying off the shelves   anyway   you're in luck   the rest is history

 Go to page 146 for the Internet Activity.

 DID YOU KNOW?
- Ian Fleming, the creator of James Bond, loved to watch birds. His character James Bond was named after an American bird-watcher.
- It's estimated that more than 2 billion people (nearly a third of the world's population) have seen a James Bond movie.

Self-Test 1: Units 1–9

A. COMPREHENSION

Circle the letter of the correct answer.

1. At the Inventors Club meetings, the members usually learn about _____.
   a. inventions that are important to society
   b. unusual but useful inventions
   c. the most important inventions in history
   d. how to become famous by inventing things

2. From the radio show, we learn that _____.
   a. different cultures have similar ideas about beauty
   b. some cultures don't care about beauty
   c. most cultures place too much importance on beauty
   d. ideas about beauty are different among cultures

3. The sultan of Brunei _____.
   a. is a rich and powerful monarch
   b. has great wealth but no power
   c. no longer has wealth or power
   d. is the powerful leader of a poor nation

4. Rites of passage _____.
   a. are a way of celebrating important holidays
   b. are tests of loyalty and bravery
   c. prepare people for changes in their lives
   d. train people to go to war

5. In South America, Percy Harrison Fawcett _____.
   a. explored places nobody had been to
   b. studied plants and animals
   c. went to war against the local people
   d. discovered a hidden city called "Z"

6. In the Northern Territory, _____.

    a. only a few crocodiles are left

    b. trained people catch dangerous crocodiles

    c. landowners don't want the Park Service to catch crocodiles on their land

    d. it is almost impossible to catch crocodiles in the wild

7. The Chinese invented _____.

    a. many things that are not useful today

    b. many beautiful things that were never useful

    c. a few things that all very important

    d. a wide variety of things, both simple and important

8. Alexander Fleming discovered how to _____.

    a. operate on infected wounds

    b. conduct trials on patients

    c. kill bacteria

    d. kill a rare disease

9. The character Precious Ramotswe is a private detective who _____.

    a. uses her formal training to help the police solve crimes

    b. is successful because she understands a lot about people

    c. is very mysterious, like the criminals she tries to find

    d. solves cases with other female detectives in her town

B. VOCABULARY

Circle the letter of the correct answer.

1. We bought a _____ for the bedroom to keep it cool in the hot weather.
   a. screen
   b. magnet
   c. fan
   d. base

2. Her _____ always looks clear and healthy.
   a. complexion
   b. features
   c. status
   d. ideals

3. Some royals are very rich, but others are not that _____.
   a. excessive
   b. affluent
   c. astounding
   d. elaborate

4. During our lifetime, most people _____ in a rite of passage.
   a. participate
   b. take place
   c. take turns
   d. were about to

5. The explorer likes to be in _____ situations where he uses his skill and strength to survive.
   a. trendy
   b. challenging
   c. brilliant
   d. mean

6. The officers at the wildlife park don't want to hurt crocodiles when they _____ them.
   a. allow
   b. occur
   c. capture
   d. support

7. That noodle dish looks so _____ that I want to eat it right now!
   a. hostile
   b. exquisite
   c. handy
   d. appetizing

8. Even today there are still many diseases like the common cold that have no _____.
   a. encounter
   b. trial
   c. spot
   d. cure

9. I love the _____ of the detective in the movie because he solved all the crimes and was a great father.
   a. role
   b. character
   c. tomb
   d. novice

C. LANGUAGE FOCUS

Circle the letter of the correct answer.

1. We _____ to the Inventors Club meeting on Tuesdays.
   a. always go
   b. go always
   c. always goes
   d. are always go

2. She has a _____ complexion.
   a. young rosy beautiful
   b. beautiful young rosy
   c. rosy beautiful young
   d. young beautiful rosy

3. The king of Thailand is _____ monarch in the world.
   a. the most wealthy
   b. the most wealthiest
   c. the wealthiest
   d. most wealthy

4. _____, she buys her wedding dress.
   a. After the ceremony takes place
   b. The ceremony takes place
   c. Before the ceremony takes place
   d. Before the ceremony took place

5. _____ Brazil?
   a. Why Fawcett explore
   b. Why Fawcett explored
   c. Why did Fawcett explored
   d. Why did Fawcett explore

6. If _____ crocodiles, it will be safer for people.
   a. the officers will catch
   b. the officers catch
   c. the officers caught
   d. catch

7. The Chinese _____ us many important things.
   a. have give
   b. have
   c. given
   d. have given

8. _____ bacteria, he discovered penicillin.
   a. When he was growing
   b. While he grew
   c. While he was growing
   d. He was growing

9. The author _____ lives in my town.
   a. who wrote the new detective book
   b. whom wrote the new detective book
   c. wrote the new detective book
   d. wrote who the new detective book

WHAT ARE SOME ENDANGERED ANIMALS?

before you listen

Answer these questions.

1. What do you think *endangered* means?
2. What animals do you think are endangered?
3. Why do you think some animals become endangered?

MEANING

🎧 *Listen to the talk. Then write the correct words in the blanks.*

alarmed	dropped	highlight	reserves
consume	habitats	mammals	wandered

1. Mountain gorillas _____, or eat, plants and fruits as the main part of their diet.

2. I was so _____ when I heard Yuki was hurt in a car accident.

3. The _____ of Jack's day was getting an A on his science paper. He worked so hard on it.

4. Endangered animals can live safely in _____; people can visit, but they can't hurt the animals.

5. Wild animals once _____, or moved around, freely all over the earth, even in places that are now big cities!

6. There are fewer polar bears in Alaska than in the past, so their numbers have _____.

7. We shouldn't separate young _____ from their families because the babies need to drink milk from their mothers.

8. Many animals are suffering because their natural _____ are getting smaller each year.

WORDS THAT GO TOGETHER

Write the correct words in the blanks.

chances of	conservation groups	endangered species

1. It is important to help _____ because they are in danger of disappearing from the earth.

2. _____ work hard to protect wildlife that is in danger.

3. Those animals' _____ survival are good because the scientists are working to protect the land where they live.

USE

Work with a partner to answer the questions. Use complete sentences.

1. To be healthy, what kinds of foods should people *consume* more of?
2. Why are *reserves* important for plants and animals?
3. What would you do if a bear *wandered* into your house?
4. When was the last time you were *alarmed* by something that happened?
5. What are two *endangered species*?
6. What will be the *highlight* of your day tomorrow?
7. What work do *conservation groups* do?
8. What are some of your favorite *mammals*?

COMPREHENSION: LONG TALK

UNDERSTANDING THE LISTENING

Listen to the talk. Then circle the correct answer.

1. Pandas are so rare because _____.
   - **a.** there are less than 2,000 living in the wild
   - **b.** they live only in China
   - **c.** there are only a few left in Chinese zoos

2. The numbers of pandas dropped to dangerous levels because _____.
   - **a.** they were all captured and put in zoos
   - **b.** they wandered out of China
   - **c.** people moved into their habitats

3. Connecting the reserves will help the pandas because _____.
   - **a.** the pandas will have more food
   - **b.** the pandas will stay in one place
   - **c.** the pandas will be closer to humans

REMEMBERING DETAILS

Listen to the talk again. Fill in the blanks.

1. Pandas live in the _____ of Central China.
2. About _____ pandas live in zoos.
3. When people moved to where the pandas lived, there was less _____ for the pandas.
4. Pandas eat between twenty and thirty pounds of bamboo every _____.
5. The Chinese are going to _____ all the panda reserves.
6. After the pandas mate, more pandas will be put back into _____.

TAKING NOTES: Endangered Animals

🎧 *Listen and write notes about the description. Which animal does it describe?*

lion

leopard

COMPREHENSION: SHORT CONVERSATIONS

🎧 *Listen to the conversations. Then circle the letter of the correct answer.*

CONVERSATION 1

1. What does the man want the woman to tell him?
   - **a.** that they're going to see wild animals
   - **b.** that there aren't any wild animals
   - **c.** what to do if they see wild animals

2. How is the woman acting toward the man?
   - **a.** She wants to make him feel better.
   - **b.** She wants to frighten him.
   - **c.** She is ignoring him.

CONVERSATION 2

3. What is the man concerned about?
   - **a.** the woman's feelings
   - **b.** the woman's speech
   - **c.** how many people will hear the speech

4. How does the woman feel about her speech?
   - **a.** concerned
   - **b.** confident
   - **c.** unhappy

CONVERSATION 3

5. Where is the woman's new job?
   - **a.** in an office
   - **b.** at a reserve
   - **c.** at a zoo

6. What is the man's opinion of zoos?
   - **a.** He thinks they're wonderful.
   - **b.** He doesn't like them.
   - **c.** He thinks the people there are mean.

DISCUSSION

Discuss the answers to these questions with your classmates.

1. There are many different endangered species. Which one interests you the most? Why?
2. How do conservation groups help wild animals?
3. What can governments do to protect their wildlife?

CRITICAL THINKING

Work with a partner. Ask each other the following questions. Discuss your answers.

1. What are the greatest dangers to wild animals today? Why are so many animals and plants in danger of disappearing? Will there be any wild animals left in the future?
2. Why do we try to save endangered species? Should we try to save them? Is it important? Why or why not?

LANGUAGE FOCUS

FUTURE WITH *WILL* AND *BE GOING TO*

Will			
I They	**will will not (won't)**	visit	the zoo.
Will	she	visit	the zoo?

Be going to			
I	**am ('m) am not ('m not)**	**going to see**	them.
He/She/It	**is ('s) is not (isn't)**		
We/You/They	**are ('re) are not (aren't)**		
Am	I	**going to see**	them?
Is	he/she/it		
Are	you/we/they		

- We use **will** or **be going to** for predictions or what we think will happen in the future.
- We use *will* for actions we decide at the moment of speaking.
- We use *be going to* for actions that we have already decided to do.

A. *Complete the sentences with the* will *or* be going to *form of the verb. Be careful. Some sentences are questions, and in other sentences both forms may be correct.*

1. Don't forget we (go) _____ to the zoo on Saturday morning at ten o'clock. We planned it two weeks ago.

2. Don't worry. I (be) _____ at the ticket office at ten o'clock.

3. You (bring) _____ your little sister with you?

4. I don't know yet. I (call) _____ and ask her now.

5. Hi Lucie. _____ you (come) _____ to the zoo with us on Saturday morning?

6. I think it (be) _____ fun for you.

7. I can't come on Saturday. I (have) _____ my first driving lesson. Remember I told you.

B. *Work with a partner. Take turns asking and answering questions about what you are going to do tomorrow.*

EXAMPLE:

A: What are you going to do tomorrow morning?

B: I'm going to be in school.

- tomorrow morning
- tomorrow afternoon
- tomorrow at noon
- tomorrow evening at 8:00

PRONUNCIATION

CONTRACTION OF *WILL*

A. *Listen and repeat the words.*

> I'll   he'll   she'll   it'll   you'll   we'll   they'll

B. *Listen and circle the letter of the sentence you hear.*

1. **a.** I'll study here.
   b. I study here.

2. **a.** We'll meet you at the restaurant.
   b. We meet you at the restaurant.

3. **a.** We'll go every day.
   b. We go every day

4. **a.** You'll tell me later.
   b. You tell me later.

(continued)

5. **a.** They'll see us.

   b. They see us.

6. **a.** You'll buy it.

   b. You buy it.

7. **a.** I'll buy that.

   b. I buy that.

8. **a.** They'll know.

   b. They know.

CONVERSATION

 A. *Listen to the conversation. Then listen again and repeat.*

Chris: What are you doing here? I thought you were going to play soccer today?

Lily: I changed my mind. I'm here to buy the Zoo Phone. It's <u>all the rage</u>.

Chris: I know. Everyone is <u>crazy about</u> it.

Lily: You should get one. It comes with pictures of endangered animals.

Chris: I know. I think they're fantastic. <u>In fact</u>, I just bought one!

Lily: Really? Well, when I get mine, it'll be <u>the highlight of</u> my day.

Do you know these expressions? What do you think they mean?

all the rage	crazy about	in fact	the highlight of

B. *Work with a partner. Practice a part of the conversation. Replace the underlined words with the words below.*

Chris: What are you doing here? I thought you were going to play soccer today?

Lily: I changed my mind. I'm here to buy the Zoo Phone. It's <u>all the rage</u>.

the latest thing   what everyone is talking about

C. Your Turn. *Write a new conversation. Use some of the words below and your own ideas. Practice the conversation with a partner.*

all the rage   crazy about   in fact   the highlight of

Go to page 146 for the Internet Activity.

DID YOU KNOW?	• Scientists believe that one species becomes extinct every twenty minutes.	

WHAT ARE SOME WAYS PEOPLE GET MARRIED?

before you listen

Answer these questions.

1. What is a popular time or place for weddings in your country?

2. Do you like to go to weddings? Why or why not?

3. What is the most unusual wedding you have ever attended? Did you like it? Why or why not?

Vocabulary

MEANING

Listen to the talk. Then write the correct words in the blanks.

adventurous	local	scary	thrilling
cramped	romantic	skyscraper	veterinarian

1. I like to shop in small _____ stores because it is good to help the store owners who live in your neighborhood.

2. My sister is very _____; she went by herself to explore rain forests in South America.

3. People who skydive say it is _____, but I would be afraid to try.

4. A lot of movies show mainly the _____ side of love, but most couples fight sometimes, too.

5. Tim's cat was sick, so he took her to the _____, and now she is getting better.

6. Amy is always afraid to go to sleep after she sees _____ movies.

7. My bedroom is very _____ because I have a lot of clothes and books, and I keep buying more!

8. The bank's office is in a tall new _____ downtown.

WORDS THAT GO TOGETHER

Write the correct words in the blanks.

exchanged vows	make the headlines	traditional wedding

1. I knew the fire would _____ because three buildings were destroyed.

2. She is having a _____ because she wants it to be just like her parents' and grandparents' ceremonies.

3. When the couple _____, they said special things and made promises to each other.

USE

Work with a partner to answer the questions. Use complete sentences.

1. What is the most *adventurous* thing you have done?

2. What makes a dinner *romantic*?

3. When and where was the last *traditional wedding* you attended?

4. What do you like to buy in *local* stores?

5. What is something *thrilling* that you would like to do?

6. What *skyscraper* do you think looks interesting?

7. How can you make more space in a *cramped* room?

8. What is something that you think is *scary*?

COMPREHENSION: LONG TALK

UNDERSTANDING THE LISTENING

Listen to the talk. Then circle the letter of the correct answer.

1. One couple got married at the Wild Animal Park because _____.

   a. they didn't have room in their office

   b. they just came back from Africa

   c. they both loved animals

2. One couple get married in a box on Fifth Avenue because _____.

   a. it went along with how they live

   b. it was very different from the way they lived

   c. they lived on Fifth Avenue

3. One couple who owned a diving school got married _____.

   a. at an aquarium

   b. under water in an ocean

   c. in their diving school

REMEMBERING DETAILS

Listen to the talk again. Circle T if the sentence is true. Circle F if the sentence is false.

1.	The talk show is on a local television station.	T	F
2.	Summer and autumn are the most popular times for weddings.	T	F
3.	One couple got married near elephants.	T	F
4.	One couple hung by ropes on the side of a building.	T	F
5.	Some weddings are so unusual that they become news stories.	T	F
6.	One couple got married on Fifth Avenue because it is very big.	T	F

TAKING NOTES: Weddings

🎧 *Listen and write notes about the description. Which person does it describe?*

judge

best man

COMPREHENSION: SHORT CONVERSATIONS

🎧 *Listen to the conversations. Then circle the letter of the correct answer.*

CONVERSATION 1

1. Where are the man and woman?

   a. at home **b.** at a restaurant **c.** outside

2. How is the man feeling?

   a. happy **b.** angry **c.** sad

CONVERSATION 2

3. What kind of wedding is the woman planning?

   a. adventurous **b.** scary **c.** traditional

4. How does the woman feel about getting married?

   a. thrilled **b.** nervous **c.** bored

CONVERSATION 3

5. When will the couple be able to move?

   a. right away **b.** in six months **c.** in a year

6. What is the man's attitude about the apartment?

   a. He accepts it the way it is. **b.** He's not happy with it. **c.** He wants to wait to move.

DISCUSSION

Discuss the answers to these questions with your classmates.

1. Which do you prefer, a traditional wedding or an unusual wedding? Why?
2. Many couples and their families spend their life savings on a wedding. Why do they do this? Should people spend a lot of money on weddings? Why or why not?
3. Why are more people today having unusual weddings? Do you think people shouldn't have unusual weddings because weddings are serious? Why or why not?

CRITICAL THINKING

Work with a partner. Ask each other the following questions. Discuss your answers.

1. What are some different feelings that brides and grooms have about their wedding? Why do many couples have arguments while planning their wedding? Do you think more couples should elope? (*Elope* means to secretly get married and tell people later.) Why or why not?
2. Marriage is a legal ceremony, but for many people, it is also a religious or a romantic one. Can you see where these three different parts of marriage could conflict with one another?

LANGUAGE FOCUS

ENOUGH AND *TOO* WITH INFINITIVES

Subject	Verb	Adjective + *Enough*	Infinitive
It	is	easy **enough**	to do.
I	am not	adventurous **enough**	to do that.

Subject	Verb	*Enough* + Noun	Infinitive
They	have	**enough** room	to have a party.
We	don't have	**enough** money	to have a big wedding.

Subject	Verb	*Too* + Adjective	Infinitive
I	am	**too** scared	to do that.
It	is	**too** far	to travel.

(continued)

- **Enough** means "sufficient." It has a positive meaning. We put *enough* after an adjective and before a noun.
- **Too** means "more than enough." It has a negative meaning. Use *too* before adjectives.

A. *Complete the sentences with* too *or* enough.

1. He was _____ worried to sleep before the wedding day.

2. They thought a traditional wedding was not exciting _____.

3. Many of their guests were _____ scared to dive under water to see the wedding.

4. At first, she thought a mid-air wedding was _____ dangerous.

5. They didn't have _____ time to plan a big wedding.

6. She wasn't brave _____ to hang from a skyscraper.

B. *Work with a partner. Take turns asking and answering questions. Use the questions below and* too *or* enough *with an adjective in your answers. Use the adjectives below or your own ideas.*

EXAMPLE:

A: Can you jump from a plane with a parachute?

B: No, I'm not brave enough to jump from a plane with a parachute.

- adventurous
- funny
- fast
- slow
- serious
- scared
- brave
- rich
- poor

1. Can you ski on a high mountain?

2. Can you make everyone in class laugh?

3. Can you take a vacation in a luxury hotel on a tropical island?

4. Can you compete in an Olympic running race?

PRONUNCIATION

VOWEL + CONSONANT SOUNDS: *tough, cough,* and *dough*

A. *Listen to the* -ough *sound in the underlined words. Listen again and repeat.*

1. They're both <u>tough</u>.

2. She shouldn't swim because she has a <u>cough</u>.

3. The cake <u>dough</u> doesn't have too much sugar.

B. *Listen to the sentences. Check the box of the -ough sound you hear.*

	tough	cough	dough
1. His research for the report was <u>thorough</u>.			
2. I'm not brave <u>enough</u>.			
3. They <u>bought</u> a new house last year.			
4. My hands feel very <u>rough</u>.			
5. He <u>thought</u> about taking that class.			
6. She <u>sought</u> advice from her friends.			

CONVERSATION

 A. *Listen to the conversation. Then listen again and repeat.*

> **Kayla:** My friends <u>tied the knot</u> today and it was just so funny.
>
> **Justin:** But didn't they have the wedding in her grandmother's house?
>
> **Kayla:** No, they didn't <u>have enough room for</u> everyone, so they had the wedding outside.
>
> **Justin:** <u>That makes sense</u>. But I still don't understand why it was funny.
>
> **Kayla:** The groom fell into the fish pond. The bride felt sorry for him, so she jumped in, too.
>
> **Justin:** <u>What a great idea</u>. In a way, it's very romantic!

Do you know these expressions? What do you think they mean?

tied the knot   have enough room for   that makes sense   what a great idea

B. *Work with a partner. Practice a part of the conversation. Replace the underlined words with the words below.*

> **Kayla:** No, <u>they didn't have enough room</u> for everyone, so they had the wedding outside.
>
> **Justin:** That makes sense. But I still don't understand why it was funny.

the space was too small   it was too crowded

C. Your Turn. *Write a new conversation. Use some of the words below and your own ideas.*
Practice the conversation with a partner.

tied the knot   have enough room for   that makes sense   what a great idea

 *Go to page 147 for the Internet Activity.*

| DID YOU KNOW? | • Companies are now offering weddings in hot-air balloons and on roller coasters 900 feet in the air.
• One of history's earliest engagement rings was given to Princess Mary, daughter of Henry VIII. She was only two years old!
• Rain on your wedding day is actually considered good luck, according to Hindu tradition. |  |

WHAT ARE SOME EXTREME SPORTS?

you listen

Answer these questions.

1. Do you like to watch the Olympics? Did you ever hear of a competition called the X Games? What do you know about it? How is it the same or different from the Olympics?

2. What do you think "extreme sports" means?

3. Which extreme sports have you heard about? If you could do any extreme sport, which would you do?

VOCABULARY

MEANING

🎧 *Listen to the talk. Then write the correct words in the blanks.*

ability	confidence	helmets	level
cliff	events	launch	perform

1. He has great musical _____ ; he plays the piano and the guitar, and he can sing!

2. At the start of the school year, the students took a test to determine their English _____.

3. The skier was at the top of the mountain and ready to _____ off the mountain.

4. We took a walk along a high _____ that looked out over the ocean.

5. The skier hurt his arm, so I hope he can _____ well at the X Games.

6. Many athletes wear _____ on their heads to protect themselves.

7. Eva has so much _____ ; she believes she can win anything.

8. Luis likes to watch all of the X Games, but his favorite _____ are snowboarding and kayaking.

WORDS THAT GO TOGETHER

Write the correct words in the blanks.

can't wait	protective gear	risk their lives

1. Construction workers have to wear the latest _____ so they don't get hurt while they are working.

2. Marta _____ to go skiing! She has never skied before and she has always wanted to do it.

3. Some people are not afraid to _____ to play extreme sports, but I wouldn't do it.

USE

Work with a partner to answer the questions. Use complete sentences.

1. Which sporting *events* do you like to attend?

2. What special *ability* do you have?

3. Where are some places where we find *cliffs*?
4. Who are two athletes who *perform* at the highest level of their sport?
5. What are some jobs in which people sometimes *risk their lives*?
6. Where is a place you *can't wait* to go?
7. What are some jobs that require workers to wear *helmets*?
8. What are some sports in which athletes wear *protective gear*?

COMPREHENSION: LONG TALK

UNDERSTANDING THE LISTENING

Listen to the talk. Then circle the letter of the correct answer.

1. There aren't more injuries than expected in extreme sports like skateboarding because _____.

   a. there aren't many athletes who participate
   b. the athletes wear equipment that protects them
   c. the skateboarders stay in the air most of the time

2. In addition to courage and skill, most extreme athletes need to have _____.
   a. a lot of friends
   b. a feeling of excitement
   c. many years of training

3. Extreme athletes need to perform at a top level because _____.
   a. one mistake can kill or seriously hurt them
   b. they don't want to look foolish
   c. they want to feel the thrill of danger

REMEMBERING DETAILS

Listen to the talk again. Answer the questions.

1. What are the names of two events in the winter X Games?
2. Where do extreme skiers launch off of?
3. Where are the skateboarders in the summer games most of the time?
4. What do all the athletes have to wear?
5. Where do extreme kayakers go?
6. What do ice and rock climbers use to hang on to rocks?

TAKING NOTES: Extreme Sports

🎧 *Listen and write notes about the description. Which sport does it describe?*

speed skating

snowboarding

COMPREHENSION: SHORT CONVERSATIONS

🎧 *Listen to the conversations. Then circle the letter of the correct answer.*

CONVERSATION 1

1. What does the man want to do?

   a. play soccer **b.** watch television **c.** go walking

2. How does the woman feel?

   a. angry **b.** sad **c.** worried

CONVERSATION 2

3. What are the man and woman about to do?

   a. go sailing on a boat **b.** go skiing **c.** fly a plane

4. How is the man feeling?

   a. excited **b.** scared **c.** tired

CONVERSATION 3

5. Who is the girl talking to?

   a. her friends **b.** a professional snowboarder **c.** her instructor

6. How is the girl feeling?

   a. She wishes she could do better. **b.** She wishes she could be with her friends. **c.** She feels she is a good snowboarder.

DISCUSSION

Discuss the answers to these questions with your classmates.

1. Why have extreme sports become so popular?
2. What kind of person does extreme sports? What personality and character traits are necessary for an extreme athlete?
3. How do you feel after you watch extreme sports? Does it make regular sports look boring? Why or why not?

CRITICAL THINKING

Work with a partner. Ask each other the following questions. Discuss your answers.

1. People expect athletes to always perform at their best, or at the "top of their game." Why is it difficult for athletes to meet those expectations? Should they always try? Why or why not?
2. People risk their lives doing extreme sports. Why do they do it? Do you think extreme sports have become too dangerous? Should people stop doing extreme sports? Why?

LANGUAGE FOCUS

MUST/MUST NOT; HAVE TO/DON'T HAVE TO

Must/Must not		
I/You/He/She/It/We/They	**must/must not**	look down.

Have to/Don't have to		
I/We/You/They	**have to/don't have to**	wear special gear.
He/She/It	**has to/doesn't have to**	wear special gear.

- We use **must** to say something is necessary or very important. We use *must* for laws, rules, or strong advice.
- We use **must not** (the negative form of *must*) when something is against the rules. It is forbidden to do it.
- We use **have to** for something that is necessary or an obligation. *Have to* is not as strong as *must*. *Have to* is the same as *need to*.
- We use **don't have to/doesn't have to** to mean something is not necessary. There is a choice.

A. *Complete the sentences with the positive or negative form of* must *or* have to.

1. You _____ wear protective gear for this sport. It is a rule.

2. You _____ finish by a certain time. It is not necessary.

3. In some countries, you _____ wear a helmet when you ride a motorcycle. It's the law.

4. You _____ talk on your cell phone when you are driving or you will have an accident.

5. He _____ have a lot of training to run a short distance. Any healthy person can run.

6. I don't think she _____ go on a special diet for this sport.

B. *Work with a partner. Take turns talking about what you* must do, have to do, *or* don't have to do *in class.*

EXAMPLE:

We must attend class every Monday and Wednesday.

We don't have to come to school on Saturdays and Sundays.

PRONUNCIATION

REDUCED FORMS OF *HAVE TO* AND *HAS TO*

A. *Listen to the sentences. Notice the reduced forms of* have to *("hafta") and* has to *("hasta"). Listen again and repeat.*

1. You have to be careful.
2. I have to work tonight.
3. Do you have to go?
4. He has to wear a helmet.
5. She has to have training.
6. It has to work.

B. *Work with a partner. Imagine that the two of you are playing a game or doing a sport together tomorrow. Take turns talking about what each of you has to do to play.*

EXAMPLE: You have to bring a baseball bat with you. You don't have to wear special clothes.

CONVERSATION

🎧 **A.** *Listen to the conversation. Then listen again and repeat.*

Kareem: I can't wait to get home. This drive is horrible.

Wanda: Yes, you have to have <u>nerves of steel</u> in this traffic.

Kareem: Well, there's <u>no room for error</u>, that's for sure.

Wanda: Everyone drives so fast. This road is like a racetrack. It scares me.

Kareem: <u>Me, too</u>. I feel as if I'm risking my life every time I get on the highway.

Wanda: <u>It's a wonder</u> we don't have to wear helmets and protective gear!

Do you know these expressions? What do you think they mean?

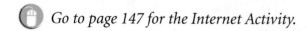

| nerves of steel | no room for error | Me, too | It's a wonder |

B. *Work with a partner. Practice a part of the conversation. Replace the underlined words with the words below.*

Kareem: Well, <u>there's no room for error</u>, that's for sure.

Wanda: Everyone drives so fast. This road is like a racetrack. It scares me.

| you have to watch what you're doing | you have to be careful |

C. Your Turn. *Write a new conversation. Use some of the words below and your own ideas. Practice the conversation with a partner.*

| nerves of steel | no room for error | Me, too | It's a wonder |

 Go to page 147 for the Internet Activity.

DID YOU KNOW?

- Extreme ironing is an activity where people iron clothing in a dangerous or remote place. Extreme ironers have already ironed on Mount Everest, the highest mountain in the world, and in Egypt's Blue Hole, one of the most dangerous places in the world to dive!

UNIT 13

WHO ARE SOME FAMOUS SCIENCE FICTION AUTHORS?

before you listen

Answer these questions.

1. What kinds of books do you like to read?
2. Who are some famous science fiction authors?
3. What are some science fiction movies you have heard about or seen?

MEADING

Listen to the talk. Then write the correct words in the blanks.

accurate	fiction	possibility	sensational
expect	immediate	predicted	technology

1. The new science fiction movie came out and was a(n) _____ success; everyone loved it right away.

2. Not long ago, computers were a new _____, but now many people use them every day at home and at work.

3. Maya is writing a report about space travel, and she has to be sure all the facts and details are _____.

4. The story in this book was really interesting, but it didn't actually happen; it is _____.

5. Joe _____ how the movie was going to end, and he was right! The scientist invented a new way for people to travel into space.

6. I'm almost finished with my research paper. I _____ to finish it today.

7. Some people believe in the _____ of life on other planets, but they aren't sure.

8. The ending of the movie was _____; the scientist found life on another planet!

WORDS THAT GO TOGETHER

Write the correct words in the blanks.

kept on	space flights	world famous

1. He is a _____ actor, so people everywhere know who he is.

2. Children are usually excited about _____ because they want to learn about the moon, the planets, and the stars.

3. Katrina _____ studying English, and soon she could speak perfectly.

USE

Work with a partner to answer the questions. Use complete sentences.

1. What kind of job do you *expect* to have later in life?
2. What is your favorite *fiction* book or movie?
3. What would like to know if you could *predict* the future?
4. What movie, television show, or song was an *immediate* success?
5. Who is a *world famous* author today?
6. What *sensational* event have you read about lately?
7. What new *technology* do you use in your daily life?
8. What do you want to *keep on* doing for the next ten years?

COMPREHENSION: LONG TALK

UNDERSTANDING THE LISTENING

Listen to the talk. Then circle the correct answer.

1. Jules Verne _____, which helped him in his writing.
   - **a.** loved reading law books
   - **b.** enjoyed reading science books
   - **c.** had a father who was a lawyer

2. Verne's books were unusual because the characters _____.
   - **a.** had adventures using unknown technology
   - **b.** had romances while they explored the world
   - **c.** became heroes on their adventures

3. Verne's predictions were amazing because _____.
   - **a.** many people had predicted new technology before
   - **b.** his predictions came from his world travels
   - **c.** many of his predictions were correct

REMEMBERING DETAILS

*Listen to the talk again. Circle **T** if the sentence is true. Circle **F** if the sentence is false.*

1. Verne's father wanted him to be a lawyer.   T   F

2. *Five Weeks in a Balloon* is about three men who explore   T   F
   South America in a balloon.

3. Scientists invented submarines fifty years after Verne wrote   T   F
   about them.

4. Verne predicted the invention of cars, subways, and cell phones.   T   F

5. In *From the Earth to the Moon*, Verne wrote about a space capsule that landed in Florida.   T   F

6. Many things that Verne said about the future were true.   T   F

TAKING NOTES: Science Fiction Authors

Listen and write notes about the description. Which author does it describe?

Jules Verne

H. G. Wells

COMPREHENSION: SHORT CONVERSATIONS

Listen to the conversations. Then circle the letter of the correct answer.

CONVERSATION 1

1. What does the woman like to do?

a. drive on the highway   **b.** travel in space   **c.** read about space travel

2. What is the man's tone of voice?

a. disappointed   **b.** unkind   **c.** scared

CONVERSATION 2

3. What can't the woman do?

a. use her phone   **b.** use her pocket PC   **c.** use her new music player

4. How is the man feeling?

a. excited   **b.** forgetful   **c.** frustrated

(continued)

5. What does the woman want to do in an hour?

    a. go to the library   **b.** study her math   **c.** go to the bookstore

6. How is the woman feeling?

    a. unhappy   **b.** confused   **c.** helpful

DISCUSSION

Discuss the answers to these questions with your classmates.

1. Why do so many people love to read science fiction? Do you like to read it? Why or why not?

2. How do you think Jules Verne was able to accurately predict so much future technology? What are some predictions for the future that you have read about recently? Do you think they will come true?

3. Which would you rather explore, the deep sea or outer space? Why? What do you think we can learn by exploring these places?

CRITICAL THINKING

Work with a partner. Ask each other the following questions. Discuss your answers.

1. Why do scientists spend a lot of time trying to predict the future? Does it help us in any way? Do you think scientists can accurately predict the future? Why or why not?

2. Some people, such as palm readers, have jobs predicting the future. Do you believe that some people can predict another person's future? Do you think people who do this are honest? Why or why not? Why do people pay others to tell them their future?

LANGUAGE FOCUS

VERB + GERUND AND VERB + INFINITIVE

A gerund or an infinitive can be the object of a verb. A **gerund** is the *-ing* form of a verb used as a noun. An **infinitive** is *to* + the base form of a verb. Some verbs are followed by a gerund, some verbs are followed by an infinitive, and some can be followed by either one.

Base form: *read*   Gerund: *reading*   Infinitive: *to read*

- Some verbs take a gerund: *enjoy, avoid, can't stand, keep on*
- Some verbs take the infinitive: *want, hope, promise, try, decide, expect, can't wait*
- Some verbs take either the gerund or the infinitive form: *love, like, hate, start, continue, prefer*

A. *Circle the correct form: gerund or infinitive. If both are correct, circle both.*

1. John enjoys (to read / reading) science fiction books.
2. People of all ages love (to watch / watching) the movie *ET* and other sci-fi movies.
3. We can't wait (to see / seeing) the next episode of the sci-fi series on television.
4. We can't avoid (to be / being) in contact with computers at some point in our daily lives.
5. He prefers (to play / playing) sci-fi video games.
6. I decided (to get / getting) my little brother a costume of his sci-fi hero.
7. As we explore space more, sci-fi stories continue (to change / changing).
8. I expect (to finish / finishing) this story soon.

B. *Work with a partner. Say four things about yourself using the verbs below followed by a gerund or an infinitive. Say three things that are true and one thing that is not true. Your partner guesses which one is not true.*

love hate like can't stand hope

EXAMPLE:

A: I love dancing. I can't stand being alone. I hate writing letters. I hope to be a scientist.

B: You don't want to be a scientist. You want to be a designer!

A: That's right!

PRONUNCIATION

REDUCED FORM OF THE INFINITIVE *TO*

A. *Listen to the sentences. Notice the reduced form of* to. *Listen again and repeat.*

1. I love to watch sci-fi movies.
2. She wants to be a writer.
3. I decided to fly in a balloon.
4. I can't wait to see the next movie.
5. He hopes to go to the moon.
6. I promised to get him the new game.

B. *Work with a partner. Take turns making and saying three sentences about yourselves with the verbs below. Use the reduced form of* to.

can't wait	expect	hope

CONVERSATION

 A. *Listen to the conversation. Then listen again and repeat.*

Mark: What do you want to do after you finish school?

Hana: I <u>would love to</u> be a world famous writer.

Mark: Really? That's great! I can't wait to read your first book.

Hana: Well, thanks. <u>Anyway</u>, what are you predicting for your future?

Mark: My father wants me to <u>follow in his footsteps</u>. He works in space technology.

Hana: Oh, that's right. He <u>practically</u> planned the next space launch!

Do you know these expressions? What do you think they mean?

would love to	anyway	follow in his footsteps	practically

B. *Work with a partner. Practice a part of the conversation. Replace the underlined words with the words below.*

Mark: My father wants me to <u>follow in his footsteps</u>. He works in space technology.

Hana: Oh, that's right. He practically invented that new moon vehicle by himself.

have a career like his	be just like him

C. Your Turn. *Write a new conversation. Use some of the words below and your own ideas. Practice the conversation with a partner.*

would love to	anyway	follow in his footsteps	practically

 Go to page 148 for the Internet Activity.

DID YOU KNOW?	• A twenty-year-old woman, Mary Shelley, created the character of Frankenstein in 1818.	

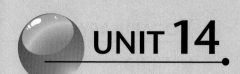

WHAT DO YOU KNOW ABOUT SLEEP?

you listen

Answer these questions.

1. How much sleep do you think you need?
2. Do many people have problems with sleep?
3. What do you do when you can't sleep?

VOCABULARY

MEANING

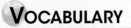 *Listen to the talk. Then write the correct words in the blanks.*

blanket	insomnia	pillows	sheets
improve	mattress	relax	snoring

1. Maria has terrible _____. She only sleeps two hours a night, and she is tired all day.

2. Liz always has an extra _____ on her bed because her room is cold.

3. The hotel workers change the _____ on the bed when a new person stays in a room.

4. Her husband was _____ so loudly that she couldn't fall asleep.

5. Many people rest their heads on _____ when they go to bed.

6. Ivan likes to sleep on a soft _____ because it makes his back and legs feel better.

7. My school grades always _____ when I eat right, study hard, and get a lot of sleep.

8. Listening to music always helps me _____. I don't think about work or school, and I just clear my mind.

WORDS THAT GO TOGETHER

Write the correct words in the blanks.

fall asleep	stay up late	waste of time

1. It was a _____ to fix the window; it broke again, and I had to buy a new one.

2. I usually _____ early after I have a busy day because I am so tired.

3. I never _____ when I have a test the next day. I need all the sleep I can get!

USE

Work with a partner to answer the questions. Use complete sentences.

1. What is something you would like to *improve*?
2. What do you think is a *waste of time*?
3. When do you *stay up* late?
4. When do you *fall asleep* early?
5. Why is *snoring* unhealthy?
6. What kind of *mattress* do you like?
7. How can people with *insomnia* help themselves go to sleep?
8. What do you do to *relax* at the end of the day?

COMPREHENSION: LONG TALK

UNDERSTANDING THE LISTENING

Listen to the talk. Then circle the letter of the correct answer.

1. The man fell asleep in the library because _____.
   - **a.** he came home late last night
   - **b.** he never goes to bed early
   - **c.** he hasn't slept for a few nights

2. Sometimes at night the man is bothered _____.
   - **a.** by the size of his bed
   - **b.** by the temperature in the bedroom
   - **c.** because he exercises too much

3. When people sleep well, _____.
   - **a.** they drive more slowly
   - **b.** they feel better
   - **c.** they don't need to exercise

REMEMBERING DETAILS

Listen to the talk again. Fill in the blanks.

1. The man is sleeping in a _____.
2. The woman thinks the man needs a nice warm _____.
3. Adults need _____ hours of sleep a night.
4. Sleep improves our _____ and memory.
5. You shouldn't drink _____ and soda late in the day.
6. You should relax for _____ before you go to bed.

TAKING NOTES: Sleep

🎧 *Listen and write notes about the description. Which situation does it describe?*

insomnia

sleepwalking

COMPREHENSION : SHORT CONVERSATIONS

🎧 *Listen to the conversations. Then circle the letter of the correct answer.*

CONVERSATION 1

1. Who is the man talking to?
   - **a.** a salesperson in a store
   - **b.** the receptionist at the hotel
   - **c.** a friend

2. How does the woman feel?
   - **a.** apologetic
   - **b.** angry
   - **c.** nervous

CONVERSATION 2

3. What beds are available?
   - **a.** one single bed
   - **b.** two single beds
   - **c.** two queen-sized beds

4. How is the man feeling?
   - **a.** upset
   - **b.** tired
   - **c.** bored

CONVERSATION 3

5. What is the woman's problem?
   - **a.** She doesn't like to eat a lot.
   - **b.** She doesn't like to sleep late.
   - **c.** She slept badly.

6. How does the woman feel?
   - **a.** She feels good.
   - **b.** She feels tired
   - **c.** Her back hurts.

DISCUSSION

A. *Find out how the students in your class sleep. Talk to three people about these questions. Complete the chart.*

Name	How many hours do you sleep?	Do you get up during the night?	Do you dream?
Karina	8	sometimes	doesn't remember

B. *Discuss the answers to these questions with your classmates.*

1. What kinds of things about a room help you to sleep better?
2. What kinds of things make you sleep badly?
3. How can your bed affect the way you sleep?

CRITICAL THINKING

Work with a partner. Ask each other the following questions. Discuss your answers.

1. What are some problems that can happen at work when people don't get enough sleep? Some companies provide workers with places to sleep for a short time. Do you think this is a good idea? Why or why not?

2. About twenty percent of Americans complain about insomnia. Why do you think so many people have difficulty sleeping? Is this a problem that comes from our modern lifestyle? Why or why not? Do you think people should take medication to help them sleep or should they do something else? Do you have any sleep remedies of your own?

LANGUAGE FOCUS

🎧 SHOULD/SHOULDN'T

You	should shouldn't (should not)	make your bed. sleep so late.

- We use **should** to say what is the best thing to do. We use **shouldn't** when it's a bad idea to do something.
- *Note: Must* is stronger than *should.* When we use *should,* we have a choice. When we use *must,* we have no choice.

A. *Read the sentences. Write advice for Tony using* should *or* shouldn't.

EXAMPLE: Tony likes to talk on the phone in bed. One night, he fell asleep on the phone and broke it!

He shouldn't talk on the phone in bed.

1. Tony goes to bed at 2:00 in the morning and gets up at 7:00. He is very tired.

   _____

2. Tony likes to sleep with the window open. Yesterday a bird flew in the open window.

   _____

3. Tony hasn't changed his sheets for one month.

   _____

4. Tony never makes his bed.

   _____

5. Tony often falls asleep on the sofa while he is watching TV.

   _____

6. Tony usually has a big meal at 10:00 in the evening and then goes to bed. He complains that he usually can't sleep for hours.

   _____

B. *Work with a partner. Take turns saying four things you* should *or* shouldn't do *to get a good night's sleep.*

EXAMPLE: You shouldn't drink coffee before you go to bed.

PRONUNCIATION

SHOULD/SHOULDN'T

 A. *Listen and circle the letter of the sentence you hear.*

1. **a.** I should buy a new bed.
   b. I shouldn't buy a new bed.
2. **a.** I should use a blanket.
   b. I shouldn't use a blanket.
3. **a.** I should close the window.
   b. I shouldn't close the window.

4. **a.** I should tell you my dream.
   b. I shouldn't tell you my dream.
5. **a.** You should make your bed.
   b. You shouldn't make your bed.
6. **a.** You should sleep late.
   b. You shouldn't sleep late.

B. *Work with a partner. Take turns saying the sentences.*

CONVERSATION

 A. *Listen to the conversation. Then listen again and repeat.*

Alan: I'm going to <u>take it easy</u> today.

Tina: <u>How come</u>?

Alan: Well, I'm very tired because I didn't sleep well all night.

Tina: Why?

Alan: I don't know. I <u>tossed and turned</u> all night.

Tina: Well, I had <u>a good night's sleep</u>, so I feel great.

Do you know these expressions? What do you think they mean?

take it easy   how come?   tossed and turned   a good night's sleep

B. *Work with a partner. Practice a part of the conversation. Replace the underlined words with the words below.*

Alan: I'm going to <u>take it easy</u> today.

Tina: How come?

take it slow   have a quiet day

C. Your Turn. *Write a new conversation. Use some of the words below and your own ideas. Practice the conversation with a partner.*

take it easy   how come?   tossed and turned   a good night's sleep

 Go to page 148 for the Internet Activity.

 DID YOU KNOW?

- The first waterbeds were made of goat skin filled with water. The Persians had waterbeds 3,800 years ago.
- Insomnia is 1.4 times more common in women than in men.
- Sleepwalking is a sleep disorder. About one in ten school-aged children sleepwalk at least once.

WHAT IS THE FUTURE OF TRANSPORTATION?

before you listen

Answer these questions.

1. What is your favorite way to travel?
2. Which type of transportation do you use the most?
3. What are some transportation problems today? How can they be solved in the future?

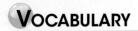VOCABULARY

MEANING

🎧 *Listen to the talk. Then write the correct words in the blanks.*

automated	destination	highways	runways
bizarre	essential	resolve	tracks

1. The train is leaving from Madrid, and its _____ is Barcelona.

2. Some subways are now _____; they don't have a person controlling them.

3. When it snows, airport workers have to clear the _____ so planes can take off and land safely.

4. Some of the cars at the "Cars of the Future" show looked _____, but they actually work better than cars we use now.

5. It is _____ that people follow the law that says they can't talk on a cell phone while they drive.

6. Many _____ get very crowded when people are driving to and from work.

7. We need to _____ the problem with the buses in our town; we need more buses at night.

8. During the storm, some tree branches fell on the train _____, so workers had to take them away.

WORDS THAT GO TOGETHER

Write the correct words in the blanks.

change lanes	look forward to	take over

1. After a long trip, I always _____ going home and seeing my family.

2. You must be careful when you _____ on a road with a lot of cars.

3. Ivan will _____ driving the bus today because John is away on vacation.

USE

Work with a partner to answer the questions. Use complete sentences.

1. What two cities in your country have *highways* that connect them?
2. What have you seen or read lately that is *bizarre*?
3. What should you do before you *change lanes* on a highway?
4. What is *essential* to your happiness?
5. What job would you like to *take over* from a friend?
6. What is an *automated* system that is part of our everyday lives?
7. What do you *look forward to*?
8. What is your favorite *destination*?

COMPREHENSION: LONG TALK

UNDERSTANDING THE LISTENING

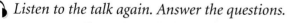

Listen to the talk. Then circle the letter of the correct answer.

1. The man and woman don't like driving to the airport because _____.
   a. it's too far away
   b. they have easier ways to travel
   c. there are too many cars on the road

2. The man thinks we need _____.
   a. more automated highways
   b. more airports
   c. better ways of transportation

3. When a car enters an automated highway _____.
   a. a computer controls it
   b. it always goes slower
   c. it goes on a track

REMEMBERING DETAILS

Listen to the talk again. Answer the questions.

1. Where is the man going?
2. Where might airports be someday?
3. Where could planes take off from?
4. What happens when you enter an automated highway?
5. What might there be between Los Angeles and New York one day?
6. How many passengers can some airplanes carry?

TAKING NOTES: Transportation

🎧 *Listen and write notes about the description. Which of the vehicles does it describe?*

station wagon

SUV

COMPREHENSION: SHORT CONVERSATIONS

🎧 *Listen to the conversations. Then circle the letter of the correct answer.*

CONVERSATION 1

1. What is the best way for the man to get to Fifth Avenue?
   a. take the subway   b. take a taxi   c. walk

2. What is the man feeling?
   a. fear   b. confusion   c. sadness

CONVERSATION 2

3. What is the problem with the train today?
   a. the engine   b. the tracks   c. the lights

4. What is the woman's tone of voice?
   a. annoyed   b. puzzled   c. bored

CONVERSATION 3

5. Where are the man and woman?
   a. in a car   b. on a train   c. on a subway

6. How is the man feeling?
   a. impatient   b. nervous   c. happy

DISCUSSION

Discuss the answers to these questions with your classmates.

1. Is it more important to build better highways or improve public transportation? Why?

2. Do you think automated highways are a good idea? What are the advantages and disadvantages?

3. Would you like to fly on a plane that carries over 800 people? Why or why not? What are the advantages and disadvantages of such large planes?

CRITICAL THINKING

Work with a partner. Ask each other the following questions. Discuss your answers.

1. What kind of future transportation would you like scientists to create? What changes in transportation do you think you might see in your lifetime?

2. What are some problems we currently have with public transportation? What improvements could be made?

LANGUAGE FOCUS

MAY, MIGHT, AND *COULD* TO EXPRESS POSSIBILITY

Subject	*May/Might/Could*	Base Form of Verb
They	may/may not	drive.
	might/might not	
	could	

- We use *may/might/could* + a base verb to express possibility now or in the future. *May*, *might*, and *could* mean "perhaps."
- For possibility, we don't use the negative form of *could*.

A. *Circle the correct word. If both words are possible, circle both.*

1. **Natalie:** John is late, and the wedding starts soon. He (could / might not) miss it.

2. **Ricardo:** Well, I don't know his flight information. It (could / might) be late.

3. **Natalie:** I (could / might) check online and find out.

(continued)

4. **Ricardo:** OK. Or he (may / could) be stuck in traffic on the way from the airport.

5. **Natalie:** Well, his flight landed on time. Hmm. He (might / could not) have gotten lost.

6. **Ricardo:** I don't think so. You (could / may) reach him on his cell phone.

7. **Natalie:** I tried but there was no answer. It (could / might not) still be turned off.

8. **Ricardo:** I hear a car. That (could / may not) be him.

B. *Work with a partner. Pam doesn't leave her house because she worries about everything. Take turns asking and answering questions about Pam using the words below. Use* may, might, *and* could *in your answers.*

EXAMPLE:

A: Why doesn't Pam take a plane to California?

B: She doesn't take a plane to California because she is afraid there might be bad weather.

Questions	Answers
1. not/drive	get stuck in traffic
2. not/take the subway	the train/stuck in a tunnel
3. not/ride a bike	hit by a car
4. not/take a bus	catch germs from other people
5. not/go by boat	get seasick

PRONUNCIATION

HOMOPHONES

Homophones are words with the same sound but a different meaning.

A. *Listen to the homophones in the sentences.*

1. My car is for **sale**. Maybe I'll **sail** around the world on a boat!

2. He bought her a **new** car. He **knew** she needed one.

B. *Listen to the sentences. For each sentence, circle the letter of the correct word.*

1. **a.** plane
   b. plain

2. **a.** bee
   b. be

3. **a.** for
   b. four

4. **a.** hour
   b. our

5. **a.** see
   b. sea

6. **a.** ate
   b. eight

C. *Work with a partner. Find homophones for these words. Then take turns making and saying new sentences.*

blew   write   whole   peace

CONVERSATION

 A. *Listen to the conversation. Then listen again and repeat.*

Danny: I saw you on the train <u>the other day</u>. Is something wrong with your car?

Clarisse: No. I ride the train sometimes to help the environment. <u>Who knows</u>, I may sell my car <u>someday</u>.

Danny: Really? That seems a bit bizarre.

Clarisse: It's not at all. I'm looking forward to a life without cars and highways.

Danny: And I really want to get a car. I might buy one <u>over the holidays</u>.

Clarisse: Well, I think I know one that's for sale!

Do you know these expressions? What do you think they mean?

the other day   who knows   someday   over the holidays

B. *Work with a partner. Practice a part of the conversation. Replace the underlined words with the words below.*

Danny: Really? That seems a bit bizarre

Clarisse: It's not at all. I'm <u>looking forward to</u> a life without cars and highways.

making plans for   dreaming of

C. Your Turn. *Write a new conversation. Use some of the words below and your own ideas. Practice the conversation with a partner.*

the other day   who knows   someday   over the holidays

Go to page 149 for the Internet Activity.

Go to page 149 for the Internet Activity.

| DID YOU KNOW? | • In 2007, British environmentalists drove 4,500 miles from Britain to Timbuktu in Africa in a truck powered by 4,000 kilograms of chocolate. |  |

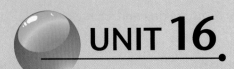

UNIT 16

WHAT ARE SOME FASCINATING STRUCTURES IN AFRICA?

you listen

Answer these questions.

1. This picture is of the Zimbabwe Ruins in Africa. What other famous structures are there in Africa?

2. The Zimbabwe Ruins are more than 550 years old. What other structures do you know around the world that are very old?

3. What are some famous structures in your country?

VOCABULARY

MEANING

Listen to the talk. Then write the correct words in the blanks.

abandoned	exactly	magnificent	piled
ancestors	fragments	material	traded

1. The market was the busiest place in town because people _____ food, clothing, and other things they needed.

2. There were a lot of dishes _____ in the kitchen sink after the party.

3. The only _____ the people used to make the structure was stones.

4. The _____ buildings are going to be torn down, and the town will build a school there.

5. The ancient palace is _____; the building itself is beautiful and the gardens and views are amazing.

6. Eli cut himself with a broken bottle, and he got small _____ of glass in his finger.

7. When we study our _____, we learn about our family's history.

8. We don't know _____ when people left this city. It was a long time ago and there is nothing written about it.

WORDS THAT GO TOGETHER

Write the correct words in the blanks.

a lack of	archaeological sites	in fact

1. My trip to Africa was wonderful; _____, it was the best trip I ever took.

2. Scientists study _____ to learn about ancient cities and cultures.

3. People suffer terribly when there is _____ water because everyone needs water to live.

USE

Work with a partner to answer the questions. Use complete sentences.

1. What *material* are most big monuments made of?

2. What do you know about your *ancestors*?

(continued)

3. What do you think is a *magnificent* structure?

4. Where are there many *archaeological* sites?

5. How can you tell the time *exactly*?

6. What do *abandoned* places often look like?

7. Where is a place in which people suffer from *a lack of* food?

8. What have you dropped that broke into *fragments*?

COMPREHENSION: LONG TALK

UNDERSTANDING THE LISTENING

Listen to the talk. Then circle the correct answer.

1. The Zimbabwe Ruins is an important archeological site because _____.
   a. it's the oldest site in the world
   b. the buildings are made only of stones
   c. the buildings are made of stones and gold

2. We know that the Zimbabweans traded with the Persians and Chinese because _____.
   a. their writings were found
   b. pieces of their pottery were found
   c. their building materials were found

3. Most historians think the people abandoned Great Zimbabwe because _____.
   a. there had many enemies
   b. they used all the building materials
   c. they didn't have enough food and firewood in the area

REMEMBERING DETAILS

Listen to the talk again. Circle T if the sentence is true. Circle F if the sentence is false.

1.	Great Zimbabwe was built between 760 and 560 years ago.	T	F
2.	Over 10,000 people lived in Great Zimbabwe.	T	F
3.	Zimbabwe means "walls of stone."	T	F
4.	The Zimbabweans traded cloth and food with the Arabs.	T	F
5.	The walls were made from small stones piled on top of each other.	T	F
6.	A thick material was used to hold the stones together.	T	F

TAKING NOTES: African Cities

Listen and write notes about the description. Which city does it describe?

Casablanca

Cairo

COMPREHENSION: SHORT CONVERSATIONS

 Listen to the conversations. Then circle the letter of the correct answer.

CONVERSATION 1

1. Why does the man doubt that the bakery has been abandoned?

   a. Bread is on the shelves.   **b.** Tables are in a corner.   **c.** Dust is on the floor.

2. What is the woman's reaction?

   a. excitement   **b.** fear   **c.** surprise

CONVERSATION 2

3. Where is the conversation taking place?

   a. in a library   **b.** in Pompeii   **c.** in a museum

4. What is the woman's attitude?

   a. annoyed   **b.** helpful   **c.** curious

CONVERSATION 3

5. What time of year is it?

   a. winter   **b.** spring   **c.** summer

6. How is the man feeling?

   a. annoyed   **b.** sad   **c.** afraid

DISCUSSION

Discuss the answers to these questions with your classmates.

1. What are some archeological sites in your country and where are they located? Have you ever visited them? Why or why not?

2. Do you think the history of Great Zimbabwe is interesting? What else would you like to know about the city?

3. Why do you think the walls at Great Zimbabwe were built so high and thick? Why do you think it was abandoned? Do you believe it was because of a lack of food? Why or why not?

CRITICAL THINKING

Work with a partner. Ask each other the following questions. Discuss your answers.

1. What do we learn by studying ancient civilizations? Did people then have any of the problems we have today?

2. Why are archeological sites important? What happens when these sites are not protected? Should they be protected by governments? Why or why not?

LANGUAGE FOCUS

PASSIVE VOICE

Passive sentences focus on the object (the person or thing receiving the action).

	Subject	**Verb**	**Object**
Active	Archaeologists	found	the city.

	Subject	**Verb**	**Agent**
Passive	The city	was found	by archaeologists.

- We form the passive with a form of *be* + past participle.
- We use the passive when we don't know who does the action, or it is not important or necessary to know who does something.

The buildings were made of stone (by people). (It is not important to say "by people.")

- We use a phrase beginning with *by* in a passive sentence to express the agent when it is important to know who does the action.

  The buildings were made by ancestors of the Zimbabwean people. (It is important to know who made the buildings.)
- We can only form the passive with transitive verbs or verbs that have an object.

  INCORRECT: Ten thousand people were lived in Great Zimbabwe. (*Lived* does not have an object, so it cannot be used in the passive)

A. *Rewrite the sentences in the passive, when possible. If the sentence cannot be made passive, write* no change.

EXAMPLE: Someone built this wall 600 years ago.

This wall was built 600 years ago.

1. We are staying in Masvingo at the moment.

   _____

2. We do not know the history of the site.

   _____

3. People believe it was the capital city of an empire.

   _____

4. People used stones to make the buildings.

   _____

5. Archaeologists found pottery at the site.

   _____

6. We went to the site yesterday.

   _____

B. *Work with a partner. Take turns making passive statements using the words below.*

- name of an event   start

EXAMPLE: The Olympic Games were started by the Greeks.

- name of a book   write
- name of a painting   paint
- name of a building   designed
- name of an invention   invent

PRONUNCIATION

CHANGE IN SYLLABIC STRESS

When we add a suffix to the end of a word, it can change the stress.

A. *Listen to the words. Then listen again and repeat.*

1. history / histORic   2. economy / ecoNOMic

B. *Underline the stress in the words. Listen and check your answers.*

1. realism / realistic   4. mystery / mysterious
2. rectangle / rectangular   5. Egypt / Egyptian
3. government / governmental   6. sympathy / sympathetic

C. *Work with a partner. Take turns saying the word pairs.*

CONVERSATION

A. *Listen to the conversation. Then listen again and repeat.*

Lorrie: Do you want to go to the Natural History Museum to see the movie about the Egyptian ruins?

Jeremy: Someone told me it wasn't very interesting. But I suppose we should go <u>see for ourselves</u>.

Lorrie: I agree. Anyway, I don't have <u>anywhere else</u> to go. By the way, isn't that museum fairly new?

Jeremy: Yes, it was built two years ago where those abandoned buildings used to be.

Lorrie: <u>Of course</u>. Now I remember. Well, I'd better go get my coat and bag.

Jeremy: OK. Meet me <u>at the foot of</u> the stairs in ten minutes.

Do you know these expressions? What do you think they mean?

see for ourselves   anywhere else   of course   at the foot of

B. *Work with a partner. Practice a part of the conversation. Replace the underlined words with the words below.*

Lorrie: I agree. Anyway, I don't have <u>anywhere else to go</u>. By the way, isn't that museum fairly new?

Jeremy: Yes, it was established two years ago. It was built where those abandoned buildings used to be.

anything else to do   any other plans

C. Your Turn. *Write a new conversation. Use some of the words below and your own ideas. Practice the conversation with a partner.*

see for ourselves   anywhere else   of course   at the foot of

Go to page 149 for the Internet Activity.

DID YOU KNOW?

- The Great Mosque at Djenné, Mali, is the largest mud structure in the world.
- The Great Sphinx in Egypt is the world's largest stone statue. It is taller than a six-story building, and has the head of a human and the body of a lion. The body and head were cut from a single limestone rock, and the paws were added on later. It has guarded the site of the pyramids for almost 4,500 years.

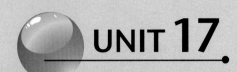

WHAT ARE THE SMALLEST COUNTRIES IN THE WORLD?

you listen

Answer these questions.

1. What are some of the largest countries in the world?

2. What are some of the smallest?

3. How do you think life is different in a very small country?

VOCABULARY

MEANING

Listen to the talk. Then write the correct words in the blanks.

attitude	barely	fountain	overcome
banned	course	gear	residents

1. I like to sit near a(n) _____ on a hot day because being near the water cools me off.

2. That race has a difficult _____ that goes through towns, up hills, and on the beach.

3. None of the _____ of this small country are poor; most people who live here are quite wealthy.

4. I have a positive _____ for this race; I really think I am going to win it!

5. She wants to _____ her fear of heights, so she is going to a restaurant on a rooftop.

6. He wants to buy new diving _____ for his vacation, but all the equipment is so expensive.

7. Ari's plane left at 1:15 and he got to the airport at 1:00. He_____ had enough time to get to the gate!

8. In many European cities there are streets where everyone walks and cars are _____.

WORDS THAT GO TOGETHER

Write the correct words in the blanks.

a bit of	be surrounded by	densely populated

1. My grandmother loves to _____ all her grandchildren.

2. My town is so _____ now that we need to build more hospitals and schools.

3. It is better to do _____ exercise than none at all.

USE

Work with a partner to answer the questions. Use complete sentences.

1. What kind of sports *gear* would you like to have?
2. Where do you often see *fountains*?
3. What is the name of a *densely populated* city?
4. What is usually along the *course* during marathon races?
5. What can you *barely* do?
6. What are some problems that people have to *overcome* in life?
7. What is something that is *banned* in your school?
8. What country are you a *resident* of?

COMPREHENSION: LONG TALK

UNDERSTANDING THE LISTENING

Listen to the talk. Then circle the letter of the correct answer.

1. The contestants have to _____.
   a. race in each of the five countries
   b. put obstacles in the way of other contestants
   c. race completely around a country

2. Team 2 feels very lucky because _____.
   a. they're racing in Central Park
   b. they're racing in a beautiful place
   c. they're racing with rich and famous people

3. People on Nauru are _____.
   a. strong and healthy
   b. agreeable and relaxed
   c. rich and happy

REMEMBERING DETAILS

Listen to the talk again. Fill in the blanks.

1. Vatican City is completely surrounded by _____.
2. Monaco is less than _____ the size of Central Park in New York City.
3. Nauru is a group of _____ in the Pacific Ocean.
4. San Marino is the _____ state in Europe.
5. In San Marino, _____ are banned from the historic center of town.
6. Liechtenstein is _____ Switzerland and Austria.

TAKING NOTES: Small Countries

Listen and write notes about the description. Which country does it describe?

Nauru

Monaco

COMPREHENSION: SHORT CONVERSATIONS

 Listen to the conversations. Then circle the letter of the correct answer.

CONVERSATION 1

1. What does the woman like about Monaco?

   a. The people are nice.   **b.** The weather is beautiful.   **c.** Everything costs a lot of money.

2. How does the man feel?

   a. curious   **b.** excited   **c.** annoyed

CONVERSATION 2

3. What does the man want the woman to do?

   a. put their clothes in the suitcases   **b.** ship their suitcases   **c.** put their gear in the suitcases

4. How does the woman feel?

   a. angry   **b.** disappointed   **c.** confused

CONVERSATION 3

5. What does the man want to do?

   a. go home   **b.** run on the beach   **c.** live on the island forever

6. How does the woman feel?

   a. concerned   **b.** nervous   **c.** happy

DISCUSSION

Discuss the answers to these questions with your classmates.

1. Is your country large or small? What are the advantages of living in a very small country? What are the disadvantages? Would you rather live in a large country or a very small country? Why?

2. What do you think life is like on a tiny island in the Pacific Ocean? Would you like to live on a small island all your life? Why or why not?

3. Would you like to live in a mountainous country, like San Marino? If not, why not? If so, would you like to live far up a mountain? Why or why not?

CRITICAL THINKING

Work with a partner. Ask each other the following questions. Discuss your answers.

1. The attitude of the people of Nauru is very relaxed. They live for today and don't worry about tomorrow. Why do you think they live that way? Can everyone feel like that? Should everyone live like that? What would happen if everyone in the world had that attitude?

2. How do the rich and famous have an effect on the places where they live? Would you like to live in a place that is filled with rich and famous people, such as Monaco? Why or why not?

LANGUAGE FOCUS

INFORMATION QUESTIONS AND NOUN CLAUSES

Information Question			Answer				
			MAIN CLAUSE		*WH-* NOUN CLAUSE		
Question Word	**Subject**	**Verb**	**Subject**	**Verb**	***wh-* Word**	**Subject**	**Verb**
Where does	he	live?	I	know	**where**	he	lives.
Why did	they	leave?	You	don't know	**why**	they	left.
When did	she	start?	He	can't remember	**when**	she	started.
What did	he	say?	We	aren't sure	**what**	he	said.
How did	you	know?	They	wonder	**how**	you	knew.

- We use **question word noun clauses** after verbs such as *know, understand, remember, wonder,* and *believe.* Most of these verbs show thinking, uncertainty, or curiosity.
- Word order in a question word noun clause is the same as a statement.

*I know where **he lives**.*

Note: To be more polite, we can use indirect questions with *can* and question word noun clauses.

Direct: Where is the station?
Indirect: Can you tell me where the station is?

A. *Complete the sentences with noun clauses.*

EXAMPLE:

A: Where is Liechtenstein?

B: I don't know *where Liechtenstein is*. _____

1. Where is San Marino?

   I don't know _____.

2. Do you know where Nauru is?

   I'm not sure _____.

3. Do you remember what he said?

   I remember _____.

4. Do you know how many people live in Monaco?

   I'm not sure _____.

5. Do you understand what I want you to do?

   I understand _____.

6. What do you want to see first?

   I'm not sure _____.

B. *Work with a partner. Take turns asking and answering polite questions for the situations below.*

EXAMPLE: • You are in a bus station. You are looking for the information desk.

A: Excuse me. Can you tell where the information desk is?

B: I'm sorry. I don't know where it is.

- You are in a department store. You are looking for the bathroom.
- You are in a new city. You are looking for the train station.
- You are in a new school. You are looking for the library.
- You are in a supermarket. You are looking for the fruits and vegetables.

PRONUNCIATION

INTONATION OF INDIRECT QUESTIONS

 A. *Listen to the questions. Where does the intonation go up? Check the box with* beginning *or* end.

	beginning	end
1. Can you tell me where the station is?		
2. Can you tell me what time it is?		
3. Can you tell me how much this is?		
4. Do you know why it's late?		
5. Do you know how to get there?		
6. Do you know where I can find one?		

B. *Work with a partner. Take turns asking the questions.*

CONVERSATION

 A. *Listen to the conversation. Then listen again and repeat.*

Sergio: Guess what? I've just <u>hit the jackpot</u>. My boss gave me a big raise.

Marie: That's great. Now you <u>don't have to worry about</u> paying for that trip to San Marino.

Sergio: Yes, there's nothing you can <u>put in my way</u> that would keep me from traveling to the place that I love.

Marie: Are you going to fly first class like the rich and famous?

Sergio: No, my raise isn't that big. But I will be able to see the village where my grandfather lived.

Marie: Wonderful! Well, you'd better <u>get ready to</u> book your flight.

Do you know these expressions? What do you think they mean?

hit the jackpot   don't have to worry about   put in my way   get ready to

B. *Work with a partner. Practice a part of the conversation. Replace the underlined words with the words below.*

Sergio: Guess what? I've <u>just hit the jackpot</u>. My boss gave me a big raise.

Marie: That's great. Now you don't have to worry about paying for that trip to San Marino.

gotten wonderful news   heard something exciting

C. Your Turn. *Write a new conversation. Use some of the words below and your own ideas. Practice the conversation with a partner.*

hit the jackpot   don't have to worry about   put in my way   get ready to

 Go to page 150 for the Internet Activity.

WHERE DO PEOPLE LIVE THE LONGEST?

before you listen

Answer these questions.

1. Who is the oldest member of your family?

2. What are some healthy places in which to live?

3. Do you think the people in your country live a healthy lifestyle? Why or why not?

VOCABULARY

MEANING

Listen to the conversation. Then write the correct words in the blanks.

active	lifestyle	scenic	sociable
factor	matter	significant	stress

1. The most important _____ for me when I move is living in a safe neighborhood.

2. People who live in small villages usually have less _____ than people who live in big noisy, crowded cities.

3. Ivan has such a busy _____; he goes to school, he works, and he is on the soccer team.

4. Being with my family and staying healthy are the two things that _____ most to me.

5. People here walk everywhere and are very _____; they never sit all day.

6. Julio is very _____; he has a lot of friends and he always wants to meet new people.

7. Your family medical history also has a(n) _____ effect on your health.

8. There's a beautiful _____ view from the end of this road.

WORDS THAT GO TOGETHER

Write the correct words in the blanks.

makes sense	natural beauty	rich in

1. It _____ that you will be happy living on a beautiful island where you have no worries.

2. I really miss the _____ of my home country; there are beautiful mountains and forests right near my mother's house.

3. Orange juice is _____ Vitamin C, so it is good to drink it to help prevent getting a cold.

USE

Work with a partner to answer the questions. Use complete sentences.

1. What is something you do to be *sociable*?
2. What is a food that is *rich in* vitamins?
3. What is something that *matters* to you in your life?
4. What is something that gives people *stress*?
5. Where is a place that has great *natural beauty*?
6. What is one *factor* you think is important to good health?
7. What do you do to be *active*?

COMPREHENSION: LONG TALK

UNDERSTANDING THE LISTENING

Listen to the talk. Then circle the letter of the orrect answer.

1. To live a long life, it is important to _____.
   a. eat about 3,000 calories a day
   b. be physically active
   c. not work too hard

2. Scientists think the secret to the longevity of Okinawans is that _____.
   a. they visit with friends a lot
   b. they live in a scenic area
   c. they eat good food

3. One reason why the people of Nicoya are healthy is that _____.
   a. they live in a large, modern city
   b. they eat lots of meat and vegetables
   c. they get a lot of exercise

REMEMBERING DETAILS

*Listen to the talk again. Circle **T** if the sentence is true. Circle **F** if the sentence is false.*

1. Lifestyle is more important to longevity than diet or environment.   T   F

2. Some Okinawans live to the age of 120.   T   F

3. Okinawans eat only about 1,500 calories a day.   T   F

4. A Mediterranean diet includes vegetables, olive oil, and red wine.   T   F

5. Nicoya is an area with a beautiful coastline, mountains, and forests.   T   F

6. The people of Nicoya have some of the stresses of living in a large city.   T   F

TAKING NOTES: Places to Live a Long Life

Listen and write notes about the description. Which place does it describe?

Sardinia, Italy

Nicoya peninsula, Costa Rica

COMPREHENSION: SHORT CONVERSATIONS

Listen to the conversations. Then circle the letter of the correct answer.

CONVERSATION 1

1. What will the couple eat tonight?

   a. vegetables   **b.** chocolate cake   **c.** meat

2. What is the woman's attitude toward the man?

   a. She's worried about him.   **b.** She's annoyed with him.   **c.** She is confused by him.

CONVERSATION 2

3. What does the man want the woman to do?

   a. get a better paying job   **b.** stop working   **c.** do work that she likes

4. How does the woman feel?

   a. stressed   **b.** sleepy   **c.** relaxed

(continued)

5. What will the man and woman see on vacation this year?

   a. monuments and museums   **b.** a big city   **c.** places in nature

6. What is the man's attitude?

   a. angry   **b.** agreeable   **c.** unsure

DISCUSSION

Discuss the answers to these questions with your classmates.

1. What features of modern life help people to be healthy? What features can cause people to be unhealthy?
2. Do you have a healthy lifestyle? What changes do you think you should make to be healthier and live longer?
3. Why do you think the people of Okinawa say that being sociable is their secret to living a long healthy life? How can seeing friends improve health?

CRITICAL THINKING

Work with a partner. Ask each other the following questions. Discuss your answers.

1. In what ways do where we live and our way of life affect our health? Since everyone can't live in a "blue zone," what parts of our environment can we control?
2. The United States is one of the richest nations in the world, but it is not one of the healthiest. Why do you think that is? How are the lives of the people you heard about in the long talk different from the lives of most Americans? What advice would you give Americans to improve their health?

LANGUAGE FOCUS

DEFINITE ARTICLE *THE*

We do not use *the* with most countries and place names.	Italy Costa Rica
We use *the* with plural place names.	the Netherlands the United Arab Emirates
We use *the* with countries that include a count noun, for example, *union, republic, states, kingdom.*	the Czech Republic the United Kingdom
We do not use *the* or *a/an* when we talk about things in general.	Diet is important for a long life. Lifestyle is important, too.
We use *the* when we talk about specific things.	The diet of the islanders is rich in vegetables and fish. The mountains in Nicoya are beautiful.

A. *Complete the sentences with* the *or* X *for no article.*

The Okinawa islands are part of _____ 1. Japan. _____ 2. islands are close to _____ 3. Taiwan and _____ 4. China. Okinanwa's capital is _____ 5. Naha. It is located on _____ 6. most populous island, _____ 7. Okinawa Island. The Okinawans' long life may be because of _____ 8. healthy diet and low-stress lifestyle they have. Their diet consists of low-fat, low-salt foods such as _____ 9. fish, tofu, and _____ 10. seaweed.

B. *Work with a partner. Take turns making and saying six sentences about the country you are living in. Be careful using* the. *Then read your sentences to each other.*

PRONUNCIATION

VOWEL SOUNDS: *LOVE* /ə/ AND *HOT* /ɑ/

A. *Listen and repeat each word.*

1. love   other   honey   won
2. hot   box   Tom   chop

	love /ə/	hot /ɑ/
1. crop		
2. Monday		
3. got		
4. done		
5. pot		
6. John		
7. nothing		
8. spot		

CONVERSATION

🎧 **A.** *Listen to the conversation. Then listen again and repeat.*

Alicia: Do you want to go to the gym with me this afternoon? I haven't exercised all week.

Bob: No, I'm <u>seeing friends</u>. We're going to play video games and then go out for burgers and fries.

Alicia: You know, you have a very unhealthy lifestyle. You need to <u>take care of</u> yourself if you want to live a long life.

Bob: I suppose you want me to eat soy all day like you do.

Alicia: Well, it's very rich in vitamins. And it's delicious, too. Anyway, my health matters to me. Actually, staying healthy <u>is at the top of my list.</u>

Bob: I suppose you're right. I'll go to the gym tomorrow. I know it's important to <u>stay active</u> if I want a long, healthy life.

Do you know these expressions? What do you think they mean?

seeing friends   take care of   is at the top of my list   stay active

B. *Work with a partner. Practice a part of the conversation. Replace the underlined words with the words below.*

> **Bob:** I suppose you want me to eat soy all day like you do.
>
> **Alicia:** Well, it's very rich in vitamins. And it's delicious, too. Anyway, my health matters to me. Actually, staying healthy <u>is at the top of my list</u>.

> couldn't be more important   is always on my mind

C. Your Turn. *Write a new conversation. Use some of the words below and your own ideas. Practice the conversation with a partner.*

> seeing friends   take care of   is at the top of my list   stay active

 Go to page 150 for the Internet Activity.

DID YOU KNOW?	• The number of people over 100 years old in Okinawa is 836, or 61 for every 100,000. In the United States, the number is 10 for every 100,000. • The average life expectancy during the Middle Ages was less than thirty years.

A. COMPREHENSION

Circle the letter of the correct answer.

1. Scientists believe that the best way to save giant pandas is to _____.
    a. keep them in zoos where they are safe
    b. give them to people to keep as pets
    c. increase land and food for them in China
    d. take them out of China and put them in protected areas in other countries

2. From the talk show, we learn that _____.
    a. most people don't want to have a traditional wedding
    b. most people like to get married during the winter
    c. people who have unusual weddings aren't serious about their marriage
    d. some people like to get married in unusual ways

3. Extreme sports athletes _____.
    a. don't usually wear protective gear
    b. don't need to have as much skill as other types of athletes
    c. usually perform their sports on television
    d. risk their lives by performing in dangerous situations

4. The characters in Jules Verne's stories _____.
    a. explored the world and used new inventions
    c. were usually real people who had accomplished great things
    b. used new ways to solve crimes
    d. were heroes who saved the world with their courage

5. Sleep is _____.
    a. something we can't change or improve
    b. very important to our health
    c. a waste of time
    d. not affected by things like beds and pillows

6. In the future, _____.

    a. people will no longer drive cars

    b. there will be changes in both personal and public ways to travel

    c. we will no longer need different forms of transportation

    d. there won't be great changes to the forms of transportation we use today

7. The Great Zimbabwe Ruins are _____.

    a. similar to the pyramids of Egypt

    b. ancient temples made from wood and bricks

    c. the remains of a city made completely of stones

    d. the ruins of an ancient pottery factory

8. The smallest countries in the world are _____.

    a. very different and far apart from one another

    b. less interesting than the larger countries

    c. all in the same area of Europe

    d. very similar in their geography

9. By studying the people who live in blue zones, we learn _____.

    a. how to make cities more beautiful

    b. how to cure illness and disease

    c. about things that make life more interesting

    d. about what helps people live a long life

B. VOCABULARY

Circle the letter of the correct answer.

1. Pandas _____ a lot of bamboo as the main part of their diet.
   a. consume   b. chase   c. wander   d. allow

2. The _____ news reporter talked to brides and grooms that live in town.
   a. infected   b. local   c. adventurous   d. charming

3. To protect their heads, extreme kayakers wear _____.
   a. reserves   b. events   c. obstacles   d. helmets

4. Millions of people read the last book in the series; it was _____ success.
   a. an immediate   b. an accurate   c. a fiction   d. a romantic

5. Your health will _____ if you get more sleep.
   a. relax   b. improve   c. attach   d. resolve

6. My final _____ is New York; that's where my meeting is.
   a. runway   b. habitat   c. destination   d. track

7. After the ancient city was _____, nobody lived there for hundreds of years.
   a. automated   b. piled   c. abandoned   d. traded

8. He wants to go fishing for the first time, so he must buy some fishing _____ first.
   a. tracks   b. fragments   c. courses   d. gear

9. Fruits and vegetables _____ in many vitamins and are very good for you.
   a. are famished   b. are surrounded by   c. make sense   d. are rich

C. LANGUAGE FOCUS

Circle the letter of the correct answer.

1. I _____ my niece to the zoo on Saturday. We planned it a week ago.
   - **a.** will take
   - **b.** am going to take
   - **c.** take
   - **d.** going to take

2. We are not _____ to have a wedding on a roller coaster.
   - **a.** adventurous enough
   - **b.** enough adventurous
   - **c.** too adventurous
   - **d.** too adventurous enough

3. He _____ finish the report by a certain time. There is no time limit.
   - **a.** must
   - **b.** must not
   - **c.** doesn't have to
   - **d.** don't have to

4. He really _____ science fiction books.
   - **a.** enjoys to read
   - **b.** enjoys to reading
   - **c.** enjoys read
   - **d.** enjoys reading

5. Coffee keeps me awake so I _____ drink it before I go to bed.
   - **a.** shouldn't
   - **b.** should
   - **c.** must
   - **d.** should not to

6. The weather is really bad so the flight _____ canceled. Let's check.
   - **a.** is
   - **b.** might be
   - **c.** may
   - **d.** might not be

7. The history of this ancient African site _____.
   - **a.** is not know
   - **b.** not known
   - **c.** is not known by people
   - **d.** is not known

8. I don't know _____.
   - **a.** Nauru is where
   - **b.** where is Nauru
   - **c.** where Nauru is
   - **d.** where Nauru

9. _____ are part of Japan.
   - **a.** Okinawa islands
   - **b.** The Okinawa islands
   - **c.** Islands Okinawa
   - **d.** An Okinawa island

APPENDICES

INTERNET ACTIVITIES

 **UNIT 1**

A. *Work in a small group. Use the Internet to learn more about two of these inventions. Answer the questions. Share your information with your classmates.*

airplane	electric light bulb	reflecting telescope	telephone
compact disk	personal computer	steam engine	

1. Who invented this item?
2. When was it invented?
3. How did the invention change the way people lived?

B. *Use the Internet to learn about two of these inventors who died poor. Answer the questions. Share your information with your classmates.*

Gridley Bryant	Janos Irinyi	Nikola Tesla
Charles Goodyear	Jan Ernst Matzeliger	

1. When did the inventor live?
2. Where did he come from?
3. What did he invent?

 **UNIT 2**

A. *Work in a small group. Use the Internet to learn about the Wodaabe people. Answer the questions. Share your information with your classmates.*

1. What ethnic group are the Wodaabe a part of?
2. Where do they live?
3. What is their main economic activity?
4. What ideals of male beauty do they believe in?
5. What do young men wear when they perform the Yaake dance to impress women that they may want to marry?

B. *Use the Internet to research one of these great beauties in history. Answer the questions. Share your information with your classmates.*

Cleopatra	Helen of Troy	Queen Nefertiti	Xishi

1. In what time and place did this woman live?
2. What are some of her characteristics?
3. Did her beauty change the world in which she lived? How?

UNIT 3

A. *Work in a small group. Use the Internet to research the monarchy in one of the countries below. Answer the questions. Share your information with your classmates.*

Japan	Jordan	Saudi Arabia	Spain	Swaziland	Thailand	Tonga

1. Who is the monarch now, and what is his or her title?
2. Who are the most famous members of the royal family and what are they known for?
3. Where does the royal family live?
4. What purpose does the royal family serve?
5. How much power does the monarch have?

B. *Use the Internet to research these famous rulers in history. Find out (1) in what country or kingdom the person ruled, (2) when the person ruled, and (3) why he or she is famous. Share your information with your classmates.*

Alexander the Great	Genghis Khan	Napoleon
Augustus Caesar	King Tut	Queen Victoria

UNIT 4

A. *Work in a small group. Use the Internet to research one of these rites of passage. Answer the questions. Share your information with your classmates.*

Australian (Aborigine) walkabout	Japanese Coming of Age Day
Burmese Shinbyu	Native American vision quest
Chinese Guan Li	Norwegian Russ ceremony

1. Who participates in the rite or ceremony?
2. At what time of life does it take place?
3. What is its purpose?
4. What do the participants do during the rite or ceremony?

B. *Use the Internet to find a traditional custom for each of the following rites of passage. Describe the custom and what country or culture it is from. Share your information with your classmates.*

birth	coming of age	funeral	retirement
birthday	engagement	graduation	wedding

UNIT 5

A. *Work in a small group. Use the Internet to research attempts to explore one of these places. Answer the questions. Share your information with your classmates.*

the Amazon rainforest	Mongolia	the Sahara
the Arabian Desert	New Guinea	the source of the Nile River
the jungles of Borneo		

1. Who is famous for exploring this place?
2. When and where did he live?
3. Did he find what he was looking for?
4. What problems did he have?
5. Did he die in the attempt?

B. *Use the Internet to learn about life in Antarctica. Find out (1) who lives there, and (2) what the weather and environment are like. Share your information with your classmates.*

UNIT 6

A. *Work in a small group. Use the Internet to research one of these dangerous jobs. Find out (1) what a worker does in the job, and (2) why it is dangerous. Share your information with your classmates.*

Alaskan crab fisherman	high-rise window washer	structural metal worker
bush pilot	snake milker	volcanologist
electrical power installer		

B. *Use the Internet to find out about life in Australia's outback. Answer the questions. Share your information with your classmates.*

1. Where is the outback located?
2. What is the environment like?
3. What is the climate like?
4. What are some of the native animals?
5. What kinds of jobs do people have there?

 **UNIT 7**

A. *Work in a small group. Use the Internet to research an ancient civilization from one of these regions. Answer the questions. Share your information with your classmates.*

Central America	the Indus Valley	Iraq	Zimbabwe
China	Iran	Turkey	

1. What was the civilization called?
2. When did the civilization exist?
3. What is it famous for?
4. Why did it disappear?

B. *Use the Internet to look up the ancient civilizations that gave us these contributions. Share your information with your classmates.*

architectural arches	the decimal system of numbers	paved roads
architectural columns	the first laws	the plow
the compass	gunpowder	the western alphabet

 **UNIT 8**

A. *Work in a small group. Use the Internet to research the life of one of these famous people in medicine. Answer the questions. Share your information with your classmates.*

Averroes	Galen	Jonas Salk
Marie Curie	Hippocrates	Andreas Vesalius
Alexander Fleming	Maimonides	Rosalyn Yallow

1. When and where did this person live?
2. What contribution did he or she make to medicine?

B. *Use the Internet to learn about natural remedies. Find and list the natural remedies for each of these problems. Share your information with your classmates.*

backache	cut	heartburn	sore throat
cold	headache	insect bite	

 **UNIT 9**

A. *Work in a small group. Use the Internet to research the famous mystery writer Agatha Christie. Answer the questions. Share your information with your classmates.*

    1. When and where was Christie born?
    2. How many crime novels did she write in her lifetime?
    3. What was Christie's nickname?
    4. Who are the two most popular detectives in Christie's novels? Give their names and describe them.

B. *Today, police departments use science to solve crimes. Use the Internet to look up "forensic science." List three ways in which the police use forensic science to solve crimes. Share your information with your classmates.*

UNIT 10

A. *Work in a small group. Use the Internet to look up one of the following nature preserves. Find out (1) the location of the preserve, (2) a description of the area, and (3) what plants and animals live there. Share your information with your classmates.*

Cano Negro National Wildlife Refuge (Costa Rica)
Gebel Elba Nature Reserve (Egypt)
Moremi Game Reserve (Botswana)
Okefenokee National Wildlife Refuge (U.S.)
Poyang Lake Nature Reserve (China)
Sariska Tiger Reserve (India)
Tubbataha Reefs Marine Park (Philippines)

B. *Use the Internet to research one of these endangered animals. Answer the questions. Share your information with your classmates.*

arctic fox	monk seal	polar bear	wolverine
lemur	mountain gorilla	snow leopard	

1. In what parts of the world does the animal live?
2. What is the animal's natural habitat?
3. Why is the animal endangered?
4. What are people doing to help this animal survive?

UNIT 11

A. *Work in a small group. Use the Internet to learn the meaning of one of these wedding customs. Share your information with your classmates.*

cutting a cake	lighting a candle	throwing the bride's bouquet
exchanging wedding rings	throwing rice	wearing white

B. *Use the Internet to research marriage customs in one of these countries. Share your information with your classmates.*

Bangladesh	El Salvador	Iran	Philippines
Brazil	Greece	Nigeria	Saudi Arabia

UNIT 12

A. *Work in a small group. Use the Internet to research one extreme sport. Answer the questions. Share your information with your classmates.*

1. What makes this sport "extreme?"
2. When and where does it take place?
3. How many people participate?
4. Is there anything dangerous about this sport?

B. *Use the Internet to look up the origins of one of these sports. Describe the sport and say when, where, and how it began. Share your information with your classmates.*

badminton	hang gliding	tepak sakraw	wind surfing
baseball	team handball	water polo	

UNIT 13

A. *Work in a small group. Use the Internet to learn about one of the following science fiction authors. Answer the questions. Share your information with your classmates.*

Ray Bradbury	Michael Crichton	George Orwell	Theodore Sturgeon
Arthur C. Clarke	C.S. Lewis	Mary Shelley	

1. When and where was the author born?
2. What is the author's most famous science fiction book?
3. What is this book about?

B. *Use the Internet to research one of these classic science fiction movies. Answer the questions. Share your information with your classmates.*

Alien	*Jurassic Park*
Armageddon	*Silent Running*
Blade Runner	*Star Wars: Episode I—The Phantom Menace*
The Incredible Shrinking Man	*2001: A Space Odyssey*

1. When did this movie come out?
2. Who directed the movie?
3. What is the story about?
4. Did you see the movie? If so, what do you think about it? If not, would you like to see it?

UNIT 14

A. *Work in a small group. Use the Internet to research different kinds of beds. Make a list of five bed types and describe each. Decide which type is your group's favorite and why. Share your information with your classmates.*

B. *Use the Internet to find out what happens when people don't get enough sleep. Also, find tips on how to sleep better. List five problems that can result from lack of sleep. Then list five tips on how to sleep better at night. Share your information with your classmates.*

 **UNIT 15**

A. *Work in a small group. Use the Internet to learn about one of these people from the early history of flight. Answer the questions. Share your information with your classmates.*

Juan de la Cierva	Henri Fabre	Harriet Quimby	Charles Kingsford Smith
Amelia Earhart	Charles Lindbergh	Helen Richey	

1. When and where did the person live?
2. What did he or she do that was special?
3. How did the person die?

B. *Use the Internet to research the history of one of these means of travel. Find out what travel was like for passengers in the early days. Share your information with your classmates.*

automobile	ship	subway (metro)	train

 **UNIT 16**

A. *Work in a small group. Use the Internet to research one of the following ancient structures in Africa. Answer the questions. Share your information with your classmates.*

Great Temple at Yeha	Pyramids of Meroe	The Walls of Benin
Palace of Husuni Kubwa	Tichitt-Walata	

1. Where is the structure located?
2. What is it?
3. When was it built and who built it?
4. What was the purpose of the structure?

B. *Use the Internet to get information about Casablanca. Answer the questions. Share your information with your classmates.*

1. Where is Casablanca located?
2. When was the city built?
3. Who settled the ancient city?
4. What was its original name?
5. Why did the city become important?
6. What is the climate in the area?
7. What is an important landmark in the city?

UNIT 17.

A. *Work in a small group. Use the Internet to learn about one of these UNESCO World Heritage Sites. Answer the questions. Share your information with your classmates.*

Aksum	Great Zimbabwe National Monument	Surtsey
Butrint	Iguazu National Park	Taxila
the Great Barrier Reef	the Old City of Dubrovnik	Timgad

1. What is a UNESCO World Heritage Site?
2. What is the purpose of the World Heritage program?
3. What is the site you researched?
4. Where is it?
5. Why is it important?

B. *Use the Internet to research one of these famous places. Answer the questions. Share your information with your classmates.*

Camelot	Cibola	Harappa	Mycenae	Troy
Carthage	El Dorado	the Lost City of Z	Shangri-la	

1. Is the place real or legendary?
2. Why is it famous?
3. If the place is real, when and where did it exist?
4. If it is not real, what stories were told about it?
5. Is there a famous person connected with the place?
6. Is there a famous book about the place?
7. Did a famous person try to find the place?

UNIT 18.

A. *Work in a small group. Use the Internet to find information about health in countries around the world. Answer two of the questions. Share your information with your classmates.*

1. Where do people live the longest?
2. Where do people live the shortest?
3. What country has the most obese (overweight) people?
4. What country has the thinnest people?
5. What are three of the healthiest countries in the world in which to live?
6. Why are the people in these countries so healthy?

B. *Use the Internet to find information on healthy foods. Find five tips (advice) on eating a healthy diet. Then make a list of ten healthy foods. Share your information with your classmates.*

MAP OF THE WORLD

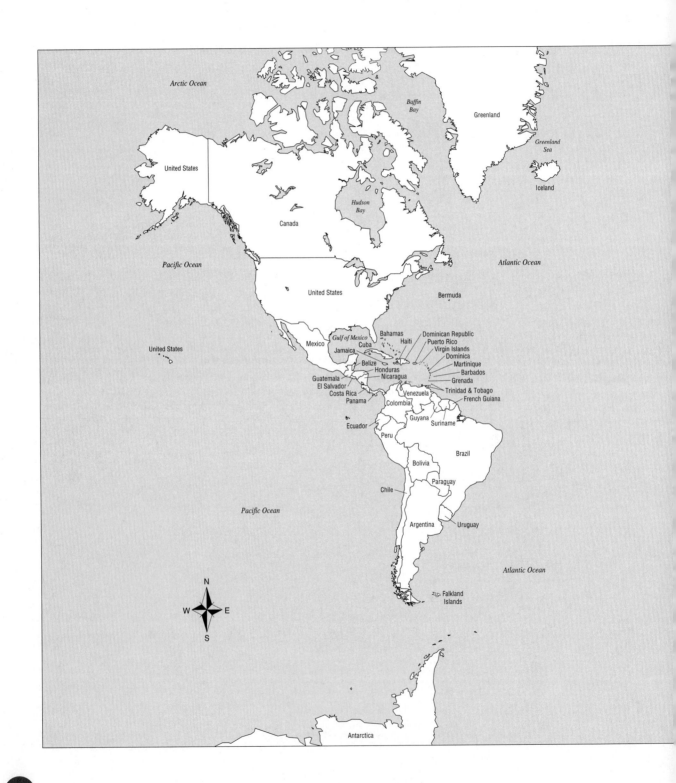

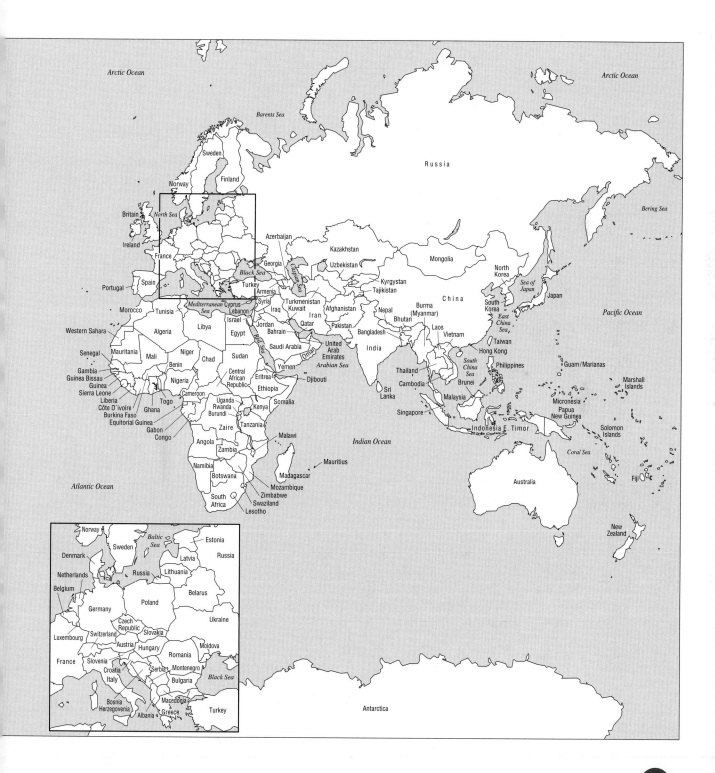